Cambridge Student Guide

Shakespeare

King Richard III

Pat Baldwin
Tom Baldwin

Series Editor: Rex Gibson

CAMBRIDGE
UNIVERSITY PRESS

PUBLISHED BY THE PRESS SYNDICATE OF THE UNIVERSITY OF CAMBRIDGE
The Pitt Building, Trumpington Street, Cambridge, United Kingdom

CAMBRIDGE UNIVERSITY PRESS
The Edinburgh Building, Cambridge CB2 2RU, UK
40 West 20th Street, New York, NY 10011–4211, USA
477 Williamstown Road, Port Melbourne, VIC 3207, Australia
Ruiz de Alarcón 13, 28014 Madrid, Spain
Dock House, The Waterfront, Cape Town 8001, South Africa

http://www.cambridge.org

First published 2002

Printed in the United Kingdom at the University Press, Cambridge

Typeface 9.5/12pt Scala   *System* QuarkXPress®

A catalogue record for this book is available from the British Library

ISBN 0 521 00812 3 paperback

Cover image: © Getty Images/PhotoDisc

Contents

Introduction

Tudor propaganda created a monster and named him Richard. His odious career began before birth, where he skulked in his mother's womb for two years. Born with teeth and shoulder-length hair, he quickly grew into a misshapen figure whose hunchback and withered arm mirrored his evil heart. He murdered all who stood in his way and pursued a vendetta against his sister-in-law Elizabeth Woodville and her ambitious brothers.

It was this monster, a fiction generated by Tudor historians to legitimise the reign of Henry VII and the Tudor dynasty, which fired Shakespeare's imagination. What sort of play did Shakespeare create? One way of thinking about the drama is to see it as Shakespeare's tale of the rise and fall of a man who will stop at nothing to become king. It is a reminder of the medieval idea of the Wheel of Fortune and the blind goddess Fortuna.

That rise–fall pattern is clearly seen in *King Richard III*. In the first three acts a charismatic Richard successfully removes anyone who stands in his way to kingship. Playing a variety of roles with malicious enjoyment, he is finally offered the crown. Yet this moment of greatest triumph heralds his downturn in fortune.

Within this structure, with its multiplicity of characters and episodes, Richard is always at the centre of attention, even when not on stage. There is no subplot or conventional romantic interest, for all events are part of Richard's rise and fall.

The play is a searching examination of power politics, but it is also an intense exploration of the nature of crime and punishment, as individuals are forced to confront past deeds. Some critics see the play as Shakespeare's dramatic interrogation of the Tudor myth (see pages 58 and 90), the final working out of the consequences of the seizure of the throne by Henry IV over eighty years before the play opens. Those events are dramatised in the plays that precede *King Richard III*. What follows is a brief summary of some of those events that will help your understanding of the play.

King Richard III is the last of four plays written by a young Shakespeare that dramatise events between 1455 and 1485: the rivalry between the supporters of King Henry VI and the house of Lancaster (who wore a red rose as their symbol) and the house of York (who wore a white rose). The important events that are frequently referred to in *King Richard III* have their beginnings in the three earlier King Henry VI plays, especially *Henry VI Part 3*. (For more details on the plays preceding *King Richard III*, see pages 68 and 74.)

Throughout the 1450s Richard, Duke of York (husband of the Duchess of York in *King Richard III*) had tried to gain control over the government of his unworldly cousin, Henry VI. The Duke was killed at the Battle of Wakefield in December 1460 by an army led by Henry VI's wife, Margaret of Anjou (Queen Margaret in *Richard III*). The Duke of York's youngest son, the seventeen-year-old Duke of Rutland, was killed in the same battle. Margaret smeared the Duke of York's face with a handkerchief dipped in his son's blood before killing him.

The three surviving sons of the Duke of York (Edward, George and Richard) became the rallying point for Yorkist supporters. A faction of nobles led by the Earl of Warwick proclaimed Edward, the eldest brother, king in March 1461. Warwick's daughter, Anne Neville, was later to become Richard's wife. The Lancastrians suffered defeat at the Battle of Towton and both Henry VI and his wife, Margaret, were forced into flight. Edward's accession was confirmed and his older brother, George, took the title of the Duke of Clarence, whilst his younger brother, Richard, became the Duke of Gloucester. Edward married a widow, Elizabeth, Lady Grey (Queen Elizabeth).

Edward's marriage infuriated powerful Warwick. He withdrew his support from Edward, allied himself with Margaret, and persuaded Clarence to join with him against his own brothers. Edward was forced into exile but Richard stayed loyal to him. Clarence, false to both sides, shifted his allegiance from his brother to Warwick, then back again.

The three brothers reunited, Edward returned triumphantly to England in 1471, reclaimed the crown and defeated and killed Warwick at the Battle of Barnet. Later in the same year Margaret was defeated and captured at the Battle of Tewkesbury. In this battle, Henry and Margaret's only son, Prince Edward, was killed by Richard. Henry VI's assassination while a prisoner in the Tower of London signalled the extinction of the house of Lancaster.

When the play opens, Richard describes the period of peace England has enjoyed under his elder brother, Edward IV, who has ruled for ten years.

Commentary

Act 1 Scene 1

King Richard III is the only Shakespeare play to begin with a soliloquy spoken by the chief protagonist. Its effect is to plunge the audience with remarkable suddenness into Richard's inner world. His deformed body hides a brilliant and witty mind, while his breathtaking honesty about himself and delight in his own cleverness quickly casts its spell over an audience. His love of intrigue and malicious plotting against those who stand in his way are evident in his opening soliloquy where, alienated and alone, he shares his innermost thoughts with the audience. The opening lines seem to celebrate an England readjusting from war to peace, but as spoken by Richard they set the tone of mocking irony that will characterise so much of the play:

> Now is the winter of our discontent
> Made glorious summer by this son of York   *(lines 1–2)*

Before the end of the scene the audience learns that 'this son of York' (Richard's brother King Edward IV) is close to death and Richard is plotting to remove all who stand in his way to England's throne. The end of the bloody civil war is to be a very brief 'summer' and present peace is to prove first fragile, then illusory. Richard caricatures the celebrations as hollow: 'stern alarums' have changed to 'merry meetings'; 'dreadful marches' have become 'delightful measures'. Described in the animal imagery that will permeate much of the play, King Edward no longer mounts horses ('barbèd steeds') but a mistress:

> He capers nimbly in a lady's chamber
> To the lascivious pleasing of a lute.   *(lines 12–13)*

Contemptuous of such frivolities, Richard begins to plot. He reflects first on his deformity. While others delight in the 'amorous looking-glass' that shows their beauty, Richard's misshapen body creates a 'shadow in the sun' that alienates him from others and their pleasures.

For Elizabethan audiences Richard's physical deformity held special significance. They viewed it as a manifestation of his inner corruption. But in modern times, how to present Richard's malformed appearance on stage or in film presents moral and practical challenges for any director. Antony Sher's Richard was distorted and misshapen, scuttling on two crutches to represent the 'bottled spider'. Other actors minimise the handicap. Sir Ian McKellen, in the film of *Richard III*, played him as only slightly handicapped and stiff-backed.

Richard himself is brutally honest about his appearance. He admits to being imperfectly shaped and blames premature birth for his condition. His defiance against everyone is expressed in the words he chooses to describe himself, in which he seems to take a deliberately perverse delight in his outward shape: he was 'cheated', 'deformed', 'unfinished', 'half made up', 'dogs bark' at him as he passes by because of his 'deformity'.

Unable to emulate the sexual exploits his brother Edward so enjoys, Richard ironically rejects the role of lover, and declares his true intention to be a villain and gain power:

> And therefore, since I cannot prove a lover
> To entertain these fair well-spoken days,
> I am determinèd to prove a villain   *(lines 28–30)*

In declaring his intention to be evil, critics find Shakespeare's portrayal of villainy resembles the character of the Vice in medieval morality plays (see page 65). The Vice was a villainous servant of the devil who trapped people into sin by charm, wit and double-dealing. The Vice often confided in the audience, encouraging them to delight in his cleverness, just as Richard now does, explaining his plot against Clarence.

He tells the audience that he has arranged for King Edward to find his brother Clarence a threat and imprison him in the Tower of London. Many of Richard's plots have a staged quality, and he often refers to plays and acting techniques, revelling in his skills as an actor throughout the play. His language further reinforces the notion of Richard the actor. 'Inductions' were dramatic prologues to plays, while he will use 'drunken prophecies, libels, and dreams' to further his scheme to have his brother murdered.

The success of Richard's plot becomes immediately evident as Clarence enters, being escorted to the Tower of London. Richard swiftly adopts the role of concerned brother, but almost all he says to Clarence is ironic. Richard does not want Clarence to have a 'good' day and knows all the answers to his questions better than his brother. His comment that Clarence should be 'new christened in the Tower' ominously forebodes what happens later in the play. (Christening uses water as a symbol of rebirth, but Clarence will shortly be drowned in a cask of wine.) Richard's 'Brother, farewell' and his promise that Clarence's imprisonment 'shall not be long' also holds sinister meaning: Clarence's imminent death.

Clarence says the king has imprisoned him in the Tower because of a prophecy: after King Edward one should reign whose name begins with a G (Clarence's forename is George). Richard, whose title also begins with G, cunningly blames his brother's confinement on the queen's influence:

> Why, this it is when men are ruled by women.
> 'Tis not the king that sends you to the Tower.   *(lines 62–3)*

Richard has in mind two women. Elizabeth had used her position as queen to gain power and influence for her large family (the Woodvilles) and in doing so had aroused much jealousy. Richard's early plotting is against the Woodvilles. He hints the queen and her brother are responsible for both Clarence's and Hastings' imprisonment.

The other woman is Jane Shore. Her name occurs frequently throughout the play, though she never appears. She is the mistress of both King Edward and Lord Hastings, and is rumoured to be a witch. Clarence hints that Hastings was responsible for keeping her out of prison. Richard accuses her of 'complaining to her deity' (King Edward or the evil spirits she was thought to worship) to secure Hastings' release.

Richard rarely misses an opportunity to mock and jeer at women. He scoffs at both Elizabeth and Jane Shore, calling them 'mighty gossips'. He refers sneeringly to the 'noble' queen who is 'Well struck in years, fair, and not jealous'. He shows his contempt for Mistress Shore by challenging Brakenbury to deny her outward beauty of 'a pretty foot, / A cherry lip, a bonny eye'. Richard often derides women through sexual innuendo: 'her delivery'; 'new-delivered Hastings'; 'nought' and 'naught' (meaning 'nothing' and 'to have sex').

In a powerfully dramatic moment illustrating the consequences of political instability and court intrigue, Clarence is escorted to the Tower as Hastings is released from it. Imprisonment and freedom will be contrasted throughout the play. Hastings is a faithful supporter of the house of York but much opposed to Queen Elizabeth and the rest of the Woodvilles. Hastings' influence weakened during the illness of his patron, King Edward, and that loss of power may have lead to his imprisonment. As he was the lover of Jane Shore, she may have been responsible for his early release.

Hastings' imagery shows that he, like Clarence, is blind to Richard's plotting:

> More pity that the eagles should be mewed
> While kites and buzzards play at liberty.   *(lines 133–4)*

'Kites and buzzards' (the Woodvilles) are inferior to 'eagles' (Clarence and Hastings) yet it is the superior birds that have been imprisoned. The image will occur twice more in the opening act. Here, Hastings fails to see that in speaking to Richard he is addressing the real bird of prey.

In his soliloquy that ends the scene, Richard reveals his brutal and evil plans with characteristic energy and humour. Imagining the future, the death of his two brothers will leave 'the world for me to bustle in!' He will marry Anne, his enemy Warwick's youngest daughter. His concluding couplet promises more intrigue, but bodes ill for Clarence and King Edward:

> Clarence still breathes, Edward still lives and reigns;
> When they are gone, then must I count my gains.

(lines 162–3)

Act 1 Scene 2

With one brother imprisoned in the Tower and another near death, Richard's next move is typically audacious: marriage to Anne, dead Warwick's youngest daughter. Directors seize the opportunity to demonstrate Richard's mesmerising power over Anne as he assumes the role of lover to the woman whose closest relatives he has just bragged of murdering: 'What though I killed her husband and her father?'

The corpse of King Henry VI is carried on stage, accompanied by the grieving Lady Anne, his intended daughter-in-law. Directors relish Lancastrian Henry VI's corpse remaining on stage throughout the scene as a potent visual symbol of past horrific deeds in the bloody civil war and Richard's particular role in them. (The body is also the play's first 'ghost', and will return in Act 5 Scene 3 to haunt Richard on the eve of his death.)

Shakespeare has altered history to suit his dramatic purpose and to increase Richard's culpability. Warwick was not killed by Richard, but died of wounds sustained during the Battle of Barnet. Prince Edward was betrothed but not married to Anne; Henry VI was Anne's *intended* father-in-law, killed by Richard after the Battle of Tewkesbury.

Anne invokes Henry's ghost to hear her 'lamentations' as she mourns the double murders of him and her husband. Her language matches the occasion: solemn, ritualistic and formal. As she grieves for 'honourable' and 'virtuous' Lancaster (King Henry) she weeps:

> Stabbed by the selfsame hand that made these wounds.
> Lo, in these windows that let forth thy life,
> I pour the helpless balm of my poor eyes. *(lines 11–13)*

Anne moves swiftly from lamenting Henry's death to cursing his killer. Her repetition of 'blood' can mean close family ties, but also gore, rage and Richard himself. Animal imagery reinforces her disgust as she wishes a fate 'More direful' on Richard than on 'wolves', 'toads' or 'any creeping venomed thing that lives'. In words that recall Richard's account of his birth, she curses not only him, but also his unborn children and any future wife. But this is deeply ironic, for it is Anne who will marry Richard and bring her own curse on herself. Anne's vulnerability is symbolised through her admission that Henry's body had been moved from the splendour of St Paul's Cathedral in London to humbler Chertsey.

Lines 33–228 are often called the wooing scene. It begins with Richard's sudden and violent entrance. In language that is the opposite to courtship he commands, then threatens, the mourners:

> Villains, set down the corpse, or by Saint Paul,
> I'll make a corpse of him that disobeys. *(lines 36–7)*

Anne's reaction to Richard combines two of the most potent Elizabethan fears: the power of the supernatural and of eternal damnation. Anne demonises Richard in her opening words to him. He is a 'fiend', 'the devil' and a 'minister of hell'. Her command to him 'Avaunt' (be gone) was accepted as an effective way of banishing supernatural beings.

Richard's cunning mind immediately turns the situation to his moral advantage. The blameless mourner (Anne) is forced to play the accuser as she invokes first superstitious belief (a murdered corpse was believed to bleed anew in the presence of the murderer); then revenge ('heav'n with lightning strike the murd'rer dead'); and finally hellish possession ('his hell-governed arm'). The guilty murderer (Richard) uses the language of forgiveness and Christian charity. Richard will use mock piety as a powerful weapon at crucial moments in the play.

The style of verbal duel between Richard and Anne (lines 68–118) is called *stichomythia*. It imitates the rapid exchanges, repetitions and contrasts found in the plays of the first-century Roman dramatist Seneca (see page 64), which were so popular at the time. Words are returned back and forth and repeated patterns of phrasing add to the rhythm of the dialogue as Anne accuses Richard of murder and he admits his bloody deeds. This quickfire repartee, with its formal and artificial qualities, was much enjoyed by Elizabethan audiences and was designed to show off the ingenious wit and intellectual cleverness of the actors and playwright. This 'keen encounter of our wits' is a formalised wooing that Shakespeare was to refine in his later comedies with the encounters of lovers such as Beatrice and Benedict in *Much Ado About Nothing*.

At this point in the play Richard's response to Anne's accusations of his cruelty is astonishing: in an outrageous move he proposes to 'lie' with Anne in her bedchamber and in a typical reversal of roles daringly blames her for his actions:

> Your beauty was the cause of that effect:
> Your beauty, that did haunt me in my sleep
> To undertake the death of all the world,
> So I might live one hour in your sweet bosom.   *(lines 126–9)*

Anne curses her beauty: 'These nails should rend that beauty from my cheeks.' She calls Richard 'homicide' (murderer) and curses him, hoping for revenge. Richard's response is to become more extravagant in his wooing as he argues it is 'most unnatural' to be revenged 'on him that loveth thee'. Richard only murdered Edward 'to help thee to a better husband'. Richard claims that though both he and Edward share the same family name, Plantagenet, he is 'one of better nature'. Anne can no longer find words to express her revulsion: she spits at him. This primitive reaction from a future queen expresses her deep disgust.

But the flamboyant actor wins the day. Delighting in wordplay, Richard's lines turn Anne's image of the eyes of a monster into his own that weep for Anne's beauty but were unable to weep at the deaths of Rutland (his murdered brother) and his father. He kneels at Anne's feet and 'lays his breast open', twice urging Anne to stab him. She cannot, and it is the scene's turning point. Anne bids Richard 'put up your sword' and is silent as Richard says:

> Vouchsafe to wear this ring.
> Look how my ring encompasseth thy finger.   *(lines 206–7)*

The ring symbolises Richard's triumph. Seizing control of events, he reveals immediately his acute grasp of the realities of power. Anne must stop mourning Henry and go to Richard's home at Crosby Place while Richard buries King Henry's body. This shrewd political move swiftly removes both Henry VI's body and Anne from public view, two potent reminders of the past that could endanger Richard's plans.

Some actors play this theatrically challenging scene as a triumph of Richard's potent sexuality and charisma, others as a symbol of the powerful male over the powerless female. Some performers bring out the grim humour behind Richard's intentions, while some actresses question whether Anne is ever completely fooled. Performers and critics continue discovering exciting and diverse interpretations of this powerful scene:

- On film, Claire Bloom was a beautiful, mature and self-confident Anne against the smouldering sexuality of Laurence Olivier's Richard.
- On stage, Antony Sher's Richard was more brutal. He expressed his deformity and sexuality by slipping his crutch under Anne's skirt.

- The poet W H Auden believed that Richard's primary satisfaction 'is the exercise of power over others against their will. Richard does not really deserve Anne: what he enjoys is successfully wooing a lady whose husband and father-in-law he has killed'.
- Peter Reynolds argues that if a slight, young and vulnerable Anne were surrounded by fourteen other actors (six pallbearers, six halberdiers, Tressel and Berkeley) Richard has not had a 'victory, but molested a child at a funeral'.

In his triumphant final soliloquy Richard revels in his success. The rhythm and energy of his lines reveal his pleasure in carrying off such a coup. Double murder has been transformed into sexual conquest. He compares his physical deformity and evil deeds to handsome Edward, scarcely believing that Anne could accept him in place of

> A sweeter and a lovelier gentleman,
> Framed in the prodigality of nature,
> Young, valiant, wise, and (no doubt) right royal,
> The spacious world cannot again afford. *(lines 246–9)*

Ironically reflecting on his faults, Richard mockingly appears to take on the qualities of the man he has murdered ('I do mistake my person all this while'). He proposes to buy a looking-glass to admire his new-found identity. Richard's final rhyming couplet is full of irony, directed principally at himself. Recalling the sun and shadow imagery of his opening soliloquy, Richard mocks the 'fair sun' and fair courtiers, identifying himself with shadows.

Act 1 Scene 3

Richard's plotting for power is contrasted with those who fear losing it. Elizabeth and the Woodvilles (Rivers is Elizabeth's brother; Grey and Dorset her sons by an earlier marriage) await news of the gravely ill King Edward. The scene will display the internal squabbling of the rival factions as the Woodvilles attempt to cling to power while Richard undermines them at every opportunity. He has already convinced Clarence and Hastings that it was Elizabeth who had them imprisoned.

Elizabeth has greater political awareness than her relatives. She understands that on Edward's death Richard would be appointed Lord

Protector of her young son. It would make Richard the most powerful person in England, and Elizabeth can see her influence waning in favour of 'A man that loves not me nor none of you'. Elizabeth probes Stanley's loyalty by reminding him that his wife, the Countess of Richmond, does not support her and also has designs on the crown. (The Countess' son by an earlier marriage will become King Henry VII.) Stanley maintains a diplomatic silence, but his allegiance will play a crucial role throughout the play. Elizabeth is not convinced when Buckingham announces that the king wishes the enmity between the Woodvilles and Richard and Hastings to end:

> Would all were well, but that will never be.
> I fear our happiness is at the height.   *(lines 40–1)*

Richard's entrance immediately dispels any hope of reconciliation as typically he carries the attack to his enemies. Hypocritically playing the role of a 'plain' man wounded by a corrupt and self-centred court, Richard launches a blistering attack on Elizabeth and the Woodvilles. He lists his grievances: they have complained to King Edward; commoners (the Woodvilles) are being ennobled beyond reason; they are the cause of Clarence's and Hastings' imprisonment.

Richard's words are full of double meanings and innuendo as he accuses Elizabeth and the Woodvilles. He claims he speaks 'simple truth' but people mistake his outward appearance. Richard expresses his resentment at 'nobility' and marriage. The high-flying eagle (Richard) is usurped by wrens (Woodvilles). Richard puns on 'noble' (meaning both 'nobility' and 'money') and 'marry' (meaning 'By the Virgin Mary' as well as 'indeed' and 'to wed').

Queen Elizabeth responds indignantly to Richard's sneering taunts against her family as old Queen Margaret enters. She is the widow of the Lancastrian King Henry VI and a bitter enemy of all King Edward's supporters. Historically, she was banished to France after the murder of her son and husband, and never returned to England. In the play, Margaret is the oldest royal survivor of the bloody civil war, and her major dramatic function will be to remind characters of their past evil acts of treachery, deceit and murder. She has much in common with the chorus in Greek tragedy, commenting on the action and expressing her viewpoint in asides to the audience. Some critics have described her as a living ghost, resurrected by Shakespeare to crystallise past events, relating them to the present as she foretells the future.

Richard's accusations against Elizabeth and her relatives are punctuated by Margaret's choric asides, which reveal Richard's past deeds. Elizabeth, Rivers, Grey (Elizabeth's first husband) and Clarence have all changed allegiances during the Wars of the Roses; Richard alone has remained loyal to the Yorkist cause. He seizes the opportunity to expose their hypocrisy while hiding behind a mask of mock simplicity: 'I am too childish-foolish for this world.'

Margaret the observer and commentator becomes Margaret the participant when she can no longer contain her anger and grief:

> Hear me, you wrangling pirates, that fall out
> In sharing that which you have pilled from me. *(lines 156–7)*

To Richard she is a 'Foul wrinkled witch'. His emotive description of a woman who first pitilessly taunted and then murdered his father unites the factions as all join in condemning Margaret's past deeds. Margaret's response is chilling. 'Can curses pierce the clouds, and enter heaven?' If they can her 'quick [living] curses' will revenge her family. The rest of the play will reveal the working out of Margaret's curses:

- Because of his excessive lifestyle, King Edward will die to pay for King Henry's murder.
- Prince Edward, the king's son, will die violently in his youth, just as Margaret's own son had died.
- Elizabeth, like Margaret, will suffer a grief-filled life without any power or status, losing her children, husband and position as queen of England.
- Rivers and Hastings will die prematurely and unexpectedly.
- Richard will be racked by conscience, suspect his friends of being traitors, and be unable to sleep for nightmares.

In the theatre, directors strive to find a visual device that will communicate the significance of Margaret's prophecies and curses while stressing their structural importance to the play. In Sam Mendes' Royal Shakespeare Company production (1992) Margaret poured a ritualistic circle of dust before pronouncing her prophecies.

During the course of the play as each awful curse came true, Margaret appeared in silhouette to repeat the words as each of Richard's victims faced death.

Richard and Margaret use similar language as they curse and accuse each other of past horrific crimes. Margaret calls Richard a 'dog', an 'elvish-marked, abortive, rooting hog' for he has murdered her husband and son. For a curse to be effective, the person cursed must be named. Richard's quick-witted interruption ensures it is Margaret who is cursed. Nothing can stop Margaret's curses becoming reality, but whether by fate or *realpolitik* (the harsh realities of power politics) is a hotly debated critical issue. Ironically, Richard himself becomes Margaret's instrument of revenge as he successively fools most of those cursed, then has them killed. He will be the final victim in the pattern of suffering and death.

Like the Greek prophetess Cassandra, who was cursed so that none believed her true prophecies, Margaret's warnings of Richard's future evil will go unheeded, with fatal consequences. The critic Derek Traversi comments that 'Margaret's exposure, however, coming from one whose life is concentrated upon the sterile savagery of the past, falls upon deaf ears in an equally savage present'. Queen Elizabeth, the 'Poor painted queen', does not see the danger of 'that bottled spider' and 'poisonous bunch-backed toad'. 'Princely Buckingham' fails to see the danger of 'dog' Richard.

Richard appears to forgive Margaret after she leaves, hypocritically hiding behind the language of religion: 'by God's holy mother', 'repent', 'God pardon'. He gloats in his soliloquy that Clarence is 'cast in darkness' and ironically quoting St Matthew's gospel in the Bible, Richard asserts 'God bids us do good for evil.' He triumphantly concludes:

> And thus I clothe my naked villainy
> With odd old ends stol'n forth of holy writ,
> And seem a saint when most I play the devil.   (*lines 336–8*)

Elizabethan audiences would perceive Richard's mock piety as blasphemy, a sin that would consign his soul to hell and everlasting suffering after death. Richard revels in his hypocrisy and superiority at fooling the inferior Woodvilles and in possessing his power of life or death over his enemies. But a contemporary audience would have seen Richard's words and actions as a profound indignity that must invoke God's wrath.

The entrance of two murderers highlights Richard's vicious behaviour while reinforcing his careful planning. The warrant is ready; they must go to Crosby Place (Richard's London home) after the murder; they must not listen to Clarence's pleas, for he can be persuasive. Richard's final dismissive command ('Go, go, dispatch') characterises his punning humour: 'dispatch' means 'to go quickly', or 'to kill'.

Act 1 Scene 4

In the Tower, Clarence recounts his dream to the Keeper. It begins with an illusory image of freedom. Escaping the Tower, Clarence flees the dangers of England, hoping to gain safety in the Yorkist sanctuary of Burgundy in France, but Richard pushes him into the sea. Drowning, he sees a fantastic vision of the worthless opulence of earthly treasure that 'mocked the dead bones that lay scattered by'. The poetic beauty of the lines, rich in classical and literary allusion, provides a striking contrast with their starkly moral message on the consequences of earthly ambition.

Having suffered the agonies of death, Clarence's tormented soul crosses the River Styx, across which the souls of the departed were said to be ferried, and reaches hell: 'the kingdom of perpetual night'. In an episode that anticipates Richard's ghostly visitors before his death at Bosworth, the ghosts of Warwick and Edward of Lancaster remind Clarence of his crimes against them and demand fitting punishment. The shrieking of the 'foul fiends' convinces Clarence he is still in hell even after he awakes.

Clarence's dream is a sustained meditation on the consequences of sin for the Christian soul, with its vision of damnation and everlasting suffering in hell for evil deeds committed in life. The episode will reverberate throughout the play as each of Richard's other victims (except for the two princes) for a brief moment, like Clarence, confronts their own moment of truth.

The realities of living in a corrupt state where princes play power games is illustrated forcefully as a principled minor character is compelled to act unethically. Brakenbury, the Lieutenant of the Tower, is forced to obey the warrant presented to him by two common murderers:

> I will not reason what is meant hereby,
> Because I will be guiltless from the meaning.   *(lines 94–5)*

The grim humour of the two murderers' prose as they debate the ethics of Clarence's murder contrasts with the poetic blank verse of Clarence's heartfelt agonising. The First Murderer is eager to perform his task but the Second Murderer feels some remorse. His literal interpretation of Christian belief would be well understood by an Elizabethan audience. He fears that on the day of judgement God will discover the sins of the dead and the souls of those who have sinned will be condemned to hell ('damned'). He has a dilemma. The warrant gives him secular authority to murder Clarence, but this will not prevent God from judging him guilty. But Shakespeare shows how such uneasy qualms of conscience are overcome at the thought of money:

FIRST MURDERER   How dost thou feel thyself now?
SECOND MURDERER   Some certain dregs of conscience are yet
      within me.
FIRST MURDERER   Remember our reward when the deed's done.
SECOND MURDERER   Come, he dies. I had forgot the reward.
                                                    (lines 117–21)

Conscience is a major theme of the play (see page 62). Characters delight in or are tortured by thoughts of their misdeeds. Both Clarence and Brakenbury have listened anxiously to their consciences, and now Shakespeare presents the murderers wrestling with their sense of right and wrong.

Clarence argues that he has not been found guilty of any crime. His words are crammed with legal terms: 'innocent', 'offence', 'accuse', 'lawful', 'judge', 'unlawful'. Clarence argues that killing him will condemn both murderers to eternal suffering. The divine law of 'The great King of kings' is above the secular power of an earthly monarch.

But Clarence is guilty of the crime he begs the murderers not to commit. Both Clarence and Richard murdered Edward, Prince of Wales, after the Battle of Tewkesbury. Clarence had perjured himself by swearing then breaking an oath to his father-in-law Warwick. The murderers' reminder to Clarence of his murder and perjury makes the First Murderer's question unanswerable:

> How canst thou urge God's dreadful law to us
> When thou hast broke it in such dear degree?   *(lines 198–9)*

Clarence argues he murdered Prince Edward for the sake of his brother and claims Richard will reward the murderers for letting him live. He cannot believe that his brother Richard wants him murdered, but the two murderers know the truth.

Clarence's final requests for mercy are answered with the double meanings that would delight Richard himself. 'Reward' means both 'financial gain' and 'fear of divine vengeance'. The murderers will go to Richard to be rewarded for Clarence's death and not his release. 'Millstones' recalls Richard's advice to the murderers, for those are what he will weep, not tears of pity. Clarence ironically believes that Richard will 'labour my delivery' for his freedom, not his death.

The murder of Clarence is the dramatic climax to the act. In one stage production, a tearful Clarence was dashed to the ground and one murderer, pricked by conscience, held out a hand to help him up while the other dealt the mortal blow. In McKellen's film, Clarence is in a bath and two soldiers brutally hold his head under the water.

The death of Clarence is the first scene without Richard, and it is the most violent. Clarence is the first of Richard's victims who suffers confinement and execution, and he faces his moment of truth as he passes from life to death. E M W Tillyard argues that 'In *Richard III* the great men die acknowledging their guilt and thinking of others'. Some critics interpret Clarence's death as a parody of Christ's last supper. Clarence is a human sop, dipped in wine by murderers who debate theology and compare their acts to Pilate.

Act 1: Critical review

Shakespeare compresses over twelve years of history into four scenes to intensify the drama of Richard's brutal rise to power. Richard swiftly establishes his character and special relationship with the audience in a bravura soliloquy. Solitary and deformed, he is unsuited to the present peaceful time. Unaffected by constraints of conscience and morality, he will be a villain.

Richard invites the audience to share in his contrariness as he employs his formidable skills against his enemies: meticulous and crafty planning; brilliant acting skills; verbal dexterity and wit; a magnetic personality; a malicious sense of humour.

Playing the roles of sympathetic brother to Clarence, ardent wooer of Anne and the virtuous man betrayed by his enemies (the Woodvilles) Richard's plots mature at breakneck speed. Clarence is imprisoned and murdered, but King Edward is blamed. Anne is wooed and won against impossible odds. Queen Elizabeth and the Woodvilles are provoked into renewed factionalism. By the act's end, Richard awaits the death of King Edward that will confirm him as Lord Protector, the most powerful man in the land.

Two women perceive Richard's true motives but are powerless to oppose him. Queen Elizabeth recognises Richard's deep hatred for herself and the Woodvilles, but her position as queen is weak, for her power and influence derives from the dying king. Queen Margaret is a more formidable opponent. Her long memory of past bloody deeds enables Shakespeare to use history to dramatise the Tudor myth (see pages 58 and 90). Richard outsmarts her as she attempts to curse him, ironically unaware that he will be the instrument of Margaret's revenge and her final victim.

Shakespeare establishes other conflicts in the act that will recur throughout the play as Richard creates disorder out of peace and pits brother against brother. Past bloody deeds resurface to haunt the present; false words and appearances conceal true thoughts and actions; imprisonment and freedom reflect political instability. That conflict is embodied in the language. The wooing scene contrasts conventional words of love against words and images of poison, blood and death. Richard is both 'saint' and 'devil'.

Act 2 Scene 1

The dying King Edward attempts to reconcile the Woodvilles (Queen Elizabeth, her son Dorset, her brother Rivers) with Hastings and Buckingham, so that his son can rule unchallenged as future king. Ignorant of Clarence's brutal murder, all on stage offer public words of friendship and unity. Edward's pious words as he appeals to each to 'swear their love' before himself and God stress his moral fallibility:

> Take heed you dally not before your king,
> Lest he that is the supreme King of kings
> Confound your hidden falsehood . . .   *(lines 12–14)*

Edward is king, but he is also a murderer and a profligate. His own bloody past confounds real hopes for reconciliation. Hastings and Rivers quickly 'swear' to 'love' each other; Elizabeth agrees only to forget her 'former hatred' of Hastings; while Dorset protests he will have an unbroken love for him. Their formal, brief, courtly words lack conviction.

Buckingham is the last to pledge his love and loyalty. The repetition of 'you and yours' rather than 'your grace' hints at his insincerity that is buried in formal rhetoric. His words are also deeply ironic because they predict his own downfall. Buckingham will betray Edward's family by joining 'hollow, treacherous' Richard, who will then betray him. By asking 'heaven' to punish him if he is disloyal, Buckingham will be another example in the play of a character whose overwhelming self-confidence brings about their downfall. As he is led to his execution (Act 5 Scene 1), he will recall the words he now speaks.

On film, productions reinforce the hollow and artificial nature of Edward's attempt to restore unity. Ian McKellen's film portrays Edward's physical incapacity. First glimpsed in an oxygen mask, he is confined to a wheelchair. His helplessness contrasts powerfully with those around him, who briefly swear allegiance as they eat and drink. Olivier's film highlights Edward's moral decline. Edward lasciviously kisses his mistress Jane Shore's hand while Elizabeth speaks.

Richard's opening words are a grotesque parody of reconciliation. Oozing superficial good humour and benevolence, he wishes for nothing but 'peace' and 'love' as he offers all present his friendship.

But his words are double-edged. Those gathered together are a 'princely heap'. Blaming 'false intelligence' and 'wrong surmise' for hostility towards him, he turns his venom on the parvenu Woodvilles. He probably speaks with contempt, sneering at Rivers' three newly acquired titles and mocking the number of titled people gathered, insisting innocently that:

> I do not know that Englishman alive
> With whom my soul is any jot at odds
> More than the infant that is born tonight.   *(lines 70–2)*

Richard neatly transforms Elizabeth's plea for Clarence to be included in the general forgiveness into general blame. He announces Clarence's death and reminds Edward that the original death warrant was never revoked, adding slyly that 'Some tardy cripple bare the countermand'. Richard throws suspicion on the Woodvilles. They are not of royal blood but murderously inclined and (like Clarence) deserve death.

Stanley kneels and begs his king to spare the life of a servant. It is an episode that ironically contrasts ceremonial forgiveness with Edward's personal responsibility for his brother's death. Edward as man and king wrestles with his dilemma as he weighs the pardoning of a self-confessed murderer against the death of his own brother. Bitter rhetorical questions and fond but spurious memories of Clarence's goodness cannot deny the inevitable conclusion: the whole family is responsible for Clarence's death. Anticipating the words of Hastings and Buckingham, Edward acknowledges the inevitability of retribution:

> Oh God, I fear thy justice will take hold
> On me and you, and mine and yours, for this.   *(lines 133–4)*

Richard's success in the power struggle may be measured from the number of lords remaining on stage as the royal party leaves. Richard cunningly hints to them that Edward's sickness and lack of judgement are 'the fruits of rashness'. He continues his vendetta against the Woodvilles, 'the guilty kindred of the queen', saying they are responsible for Clarence's death.

Act 2 Scene 2

Clarence's two children question their grandmother (the Duchess of York) about their father's death. She attempts vainly to protect them from the truth (protesting that she weeps for Edward's illness, not Clarence's death) but her lie is quickly exposed. Richard has already corrupted the minds of these 'Incapable and shallow innocents' by making them believe Edward and the Woodvilles are responsible for their father's murder.

Some critics believe Clarence's children contribute to the pathos of the play. They hauntingly prefigure the isolation and murder of their more famous cousins (the princes in the Tower). Like them, they are children deceived by Uncle Richard's words and appearance. The naive boy refuses to believe his grandmother's judgement of her son who can 'with a virtuous visor hide deep vice'. Other critics declare Clarence's children less innocent. Their father's murder links them inextricably to the cycle of violence and retribution in a scene that begins with a lie and ends in profound deceit. Both children demonstrate their inherited taste for revenge as the boy repeats chillingly Richard's line from the previous scene 'God will revenge it', which is speedily affirmed by his sister.

Elizabeth's sudden entrance deepens the mood of tragic loss. Two children are fatherless, Elizabeth is now a widow and the Duchess is left to grieve the death of two sons. Individual grief is transformed into shared suffering as all characters mourn their loss.

The Duchess and Elizabeth first express their profound suffering through metaphor. The 'branches' and 'root' are images of the family tree of King Edward, a tree that will now die. The 'two mirrors' are the Duchess of York's sons, Edward and Clarence, and the 'false glass' is Richard. With Edward and Clarence dead, her support – 'two crutches' – has gone. Queen Elizabeth asks for her eyes to be like the ocean so she may flood the world with her tears.

Finally all lament in formal, ritualistic language, repeated words and phrases heightening emotional intensity and dramatic effect:

ELIZABETH   Was never widow had so dear a loss.
CHILDREN   Were never orphans had so dear a loss.   *(lines 77–8)*

Here, Shakespeare's use of formal, stylised language shows the influence of the first-century Roman playwright Seneca. Such language reinforces the drama in key episodes (Anne's wooing, the scenes of lamentation, Margaret's prophecies). Frank Kermode refers to this passage as 'an operatic chorus'. He judges it splendid, but admits it 'belongs to the earliest phase of Shakespeare's work'. To Tillyard the 'obvious antiphony' (response) is an 'incantation'. Some present-day directors view the passages of sustained choric lamentation as too melodramatic for contemporary taste, emphasising the repetitions for comic effect.

The Woodville men respond very differently. Dorset reminds his mother of the Christian belief of the power of God over human life. Elizabeth's brother Rivers fears Edward's death has created a power vacuum that must be filled immediately. Urging that Elizabeth's young son must be crowned at once, Rivers' words repeat the image of a strong family tree:

> And plant your joys in living Edward's throne.   *(line 100)*

Richard's entrance disperses the grief-laden atmosphere. He expresses brief condolences to Elizabeth ('Sister, have comfort') and comments on his mother's benediction with a sarcastic aside. It is the 'butt-end of a mother's blessing'.

Buckingham argues that a small escort should bring Prince Edward from Ludlow Castle to London for his coronation, as a large entourage might provoke unrest. Images of growth and unity have an ominous ring. 'We are to reap the harvest of his son' echoes Richard's boast that he has 'cropped the golden prime' of Prince Edward (Act 1 Scene 2, line 251). The power struggle in the kingdom is fragile; 'the estate is green', but 'green' carries further meaning of a country ruled under Edward's minority being tender and easily damaged. Buckingham's prepared speech, with its formal rhetoric and complex syntax, seems to persuade the Woodvilles to accept his proposal.

Richard and Buckingham's true intention becomes clear when they are alone. The first part of their plan is to isolate 'the queen's proud kindred from the prince'. Richard's language illustrates the two contrasting characteristics of the Vice in morality plays – as he flatters Buckingham he is seemingly innocuous but in reality is duplicitous. He and Buckingham are utterly alike ('My other self') and think as one ('my counsel's consistory'). From this point, Buckingham will be Richard's partner in crime.

Act 2 Scene 3

Shakespeare now provides a brief expression of the views of the ordinary people of the land. Three citizens discuss the consequences of Edward's death. The Second and Third Citizens have a very pessimistic view of a future England under the rule of the young Prince Edward.

The Third Citizen remembers the disastrous wars against France and bloody civil strife under young King Henry VI as he declares 'Woe to that land that's governed by a child.' The Second Citizen sees some hope that Edward will govern wisely, though only a child ('in his nonage'). But the Third Citizen expresses the stronger argument. The Duke of Gloucester is dangerous and the Woodvilles are proud and unfit to rule. England will only be saved if it is the will of God. Men's hearts are fearful. The 'divine instinct' that enables men's minds to recognise approaching danger lives in ordinary people, who seem to possess a wisdom denied to the nobility.

Although it was Elizabethan dramatic convention for low-status characters to use prose, the citizens speak in stylised and formal verse. Their mixture of commonplace truisms, received wisdom, and biblical example add gravitas to their shrewd political judgements. The critic Frank Kermode points to their language having an 'archaic force' and their words 'seem to derive from a sort of shared dialect, and nobody sees any harm in making a point several times over, with some elegance of illustration'.

Act 2 Scene 4

Three generations of the house of York await the arrival of Prince Edward, who is travelling from Ludlow to London for his coronation. The Archbishop reports on the young prince's journey and his expected day of arrival, while the Duchess hopes he is 'much grown'. This domestic family scene ironically contrasts with the political reality of the pessimistic citizens and their apprehensive prophecies, and Richard and Buckingham's plot to isolate the Woodvilles from Prince Edward.

The tone becomes more sinister with the mention of 'my uncle Gloucester'. The young Duke of York does not want to outgrow his brother because Richard had equated rapid physical growth with weeds and slow development with moral excellence: '"Small herbs have grace; great weeds do grow apace."' But the Duchess remembers Richard's own slow growth:

He was the wretched'st thing when he was young,
So long a-growing, and so leisurely,
That if his rule were true, he should be gracious.   *(lines 18–20)*

But grandson challenges grandmother's memory. 'Marry, they say' (York cannot be more precise) that Richard grew so fast that he could 'gnaw a crust at two hours old'. Mischievous York uses rumour to uncover a truth, but is ironically unaware of its meaning. Richard is truly a malignant, fast-growing weed and the infant with teeth. He is the monster who will devour the princes before they grow in stature or goodness.

A messenger brings news of the arrest and imprisonment of Elizabeth's son (Grey), brother (Rivers) and supporter Sir Thomas Vaughan on the orders of Richard and Buckingham. Their offence is 'all unknown'. The bad news is delivered in short, sharp phrases and sentences, which contrast with Elizabeth's sustained outcry in which she sees the destruction of her family. The 'tiger' (Richard) seizes 'the gentle hind' (Prince Edward) and it is 'the end of all'.

The Duchess describes her conflicting emotions at her husband's death and her sons' defeats and victories. Repeated words, phrases, rhythms and sounds give great dramatic force to her plea for the cycle of killing to end: 'brother to brother, / Blood to blood, self against self'.

Elizabeth seeks sanctuary with her son. In medieval times, Church law guaranteed that a fugitive from justice or debt was immune from arrest if they sought sanctuary in a church or other sacred place. The Archbishop hands over the 'seal' of England, the symbol of sovereignty. The future destiny of England rests now with children and a powerless woman who is all too aware that Richard intends them harm.

Act 2: Critical review

The opening scene portrays a king desperate to negotiate a secure future for his family by uniting the warring factions that threaten the peace and stability of the kingdom. By the end of the act, both King Edward and his hopes of future peace are dead, and England is plunged into political turmoil.

Richard's brilliant exploitation of his enemies' weaknesses has enabled him to accomplish that momentous change swiftly and ruthlessly. Throughout the act, Richard's schemes to gain power provide a vivid and powerful contrast to the divided and weak royal household. Exploiting Edward's weaknesses, Richard cynically uses Clarence's death to his advantage by throwing suspicion on his enemies. With the reopening of old wounds, Richard acts.

His plans are brutal and devastating, and he shares them with the able and clever Buckingham. The two men will sweep aside all opposition until Richard gains the throne. The two plot to separate the young king from his family; Queen Elizabeth and her remaining son are forced into sanctuary; the Duchess of York is compelled to join them. Of the eight speaking characters Edward addresses in the opening scene, only two (Stanley and Queen Elizabeth) will live to see Richmond crowned.

Richard's march to power seems inevitable, but one scene puts an essential perspective on his manoeuvring for the crown. Three citizens voice their fears for the future of a land ruled by Richard. It is one of only two scenes in the play (the other is the Scrivener's in Act 3 Scene 6) when ordinary citizens voice their opinion without the presence of high-status characters. The citizens put their trust in God to rescue the kingdom, but their powerlessness to act reveals the extent of Richard's *realpolitik*.

Richard exerts enormous influence throughout the act, but he appears in only two of the four scenes. The mocking, often ominous humour that so characterised his earlier appearances is limited to only two instances (his insincere plea for amity in Scene 1 lines 58–61; his aside to the Duchess in Scene 2 lines 109–11). Much of the language of the act reflects the dangerous political situation, with frequent references to grief, suffering, loss and death.

Act 3 Scene 1

Young Prince Edward ceremoniously enters London as king-in-waiting. But Richard's words of greeting ('Welcome, dear cousin, my thoughts' sovereign') means both 'king of my thoughts' and 'my overriding thought of your death', establishing instantly Richard's murderous intentions and Edward's vulnerability. Edward is isolated and 'melancholy', with his mother and brother in sanctuary, uncles arrested and family friend Hastings late.

Richard cunningly justifies the arrests of Rivers and Grey by adopting the same tactics he accuses them of using on Edward. The prince must not be fooled by their 'outward show' for they were 'dangerous', used 'sugared words' and were 'false friends'. Richard's deceitful words do not convince Edward, who believes in his uncles (for they are not 'false friends').

The confrontation between the Cardinal and Buckingham on the right of sanctuary is prompted by Hastings' statement that Elizabeth will not release the Duke of York to meet his brother Edward. Buckingham argues she must release the boy; if she will not be persuaded, Hastings must 'pluck him perforce' from her 'jealous arms'. The Cardinal refuses to break the 'holy privilege / Of blessèd sanctuary' but Buckingham will not be denied:

> You are too senseless obstinate, my lord,
> Too ceremonious and traditional.
> Weigh it but with the grossness of this age   *(lines 44–6)*

Buckingham's words herald the beginning of a new order, where persuasion must give way to force and opposition is 'peevish'. His dismissive words on 'sanctuary children' often cause laughter in the theatre, but reveal contempt for the Church and its protection of the innocent and vulnerable. In the new world Buckingham foresees, tension between Church and state is inevitable (see page 63).

Richard's suggestion that Edward 'repose' in the Tower meets with an unequivocal response: 'I do not like the Tower, of any place.' The Tower of London symbolised oppression, a place of imprisonment and death without regard for status (see page 72). Here, Shakespeare also uses it as an occasion for Edward to reflect on the nature of history and truth following Buckingham's two untruths about the Tower's beginnings (the Tower was not built by

Caesar, but that was the accepted Elizabethan myth). Edward asserts that truth comes from both written records ('registered') and oral tradition ('retailed') but however recorded 'the truth should live from age to age'. Edward praises Julius Caesar, who was brave and recorded his own deeds for posterity. Edward wishes to emulate Caesar and become a heroic figure in England's history.

But Richard's three asides mockingly reveal Edward's true place in history. He will not live, so his youthful valour will never rekindle England's heroic past. The irony of his lines is deepened further by Edward's comments on Caesar. Just as trusted associates murdered Caesar, so Edward will be murdered on the orders of a trusted uncle. His death will plunge England into civil strife just as Rome disintegrated after Caesar's assassination.

The episode reflects Shakespeare's interest in an important contemporary issue: what constitutes historical truth. Oral tradition is unreliable and is not proof, so there is a need for reliable written evidence. Shakespeare was all too aware of writing a version of history that was often far from truthful (see page 60).

The two princes are united and York mischievously reminds Richard of his earlier words:

- Edward has outgrown York, so the future king is a useless ('idle') weed.
- York identifies Richard with the Vice, his hand always on his dagger. York's request for a 'dagger', 'sword' and 'weapon' reminds an audience that they are gifts that bring death. 'My dagger, little cousin? With all my heart' stresses Richard's murderous desire to plunge the dagger into York's heart.
- Puns on 'light', 'weightier' and 'bear' have sinister double meanings (for example 'bear' can mean both 'to carry' but also 'to tolerate').
- York caricatures his uncle as the grotesque hunchback with himself the ape on Richard's shoulders (trained bears carried apes on their shoulders, which made them look hunchbacked).

On stage, at this moment Antony Sher as Richard turned away from the princes, then diffused the tension by imitating an ape. Henry Irving as Richard glared silently in concentrated hatred. On film, both Olivier and McKellen have York leap onto their shoulders, causing Richard to lose control in a moment of pain and anger. Some productions portray York as a miniature Richard, possessing many of his uncle's qualities: 'Bold, quick, ingenious, forward, capable'.

The departure of the princes for the Tower is the last time they appear alive in the play. The mood of foreboding is heightened by the repeated references to the Tower, York's fear of Clarence's ghost, and Edward's thought of the possible fate of Grey and Rivers:

> And if they live, I hope I need not fear.
> But come, my lord, and with a heavy heart,
> Thinking on them, go I unto the Tower.　　　　*(lines 149–51)*

Hastings' loyalty to Richard is to be tested. Buckingham is politic and subtle as he instructs Catesby to judge Hastings' position 'as it were far off', but Richard's message to Hastings is typically ambiguous. Outwardly bringing him good news (his enemies will be killed and he can rejoice with his mistress), it is also sinister and threatening (what can happen to his enemies can happen to him and Richard is aware of Hastings' sexual indiscretions). Richard will use Mistress Shore as the means of Hastings' downfall (Act 3 Scene 4). Richard's brutality is sharply revealed in his response to Buckingham's query about what to do if Hastings does not comply: 'Chop off his head.'

Richard cannot resist further clever wordplay as he celebrates the success of his secret plans. Promising to reward Buckingham for his loyalty, when he is king Richard will offer his friend the earldom of Hereford 'with all kindness'. Richard's pun on 'kindness' can mean 'generosity', but also means 'according to his nature', which carries sinister implications for Buckingham.

Act 3 Scene 2

The scene reveals the naivety and arrogance of Hastings, a faithful supporter of King Edward's sons. His over-confidence and blindness to the real motives of others, allied to his bitter opposition to the Woodvilles, make him an easy victim for Richard's plans. His misinterpretations of every warning create both humour and grim irony as successively throughout the scene he encounters a friend (Stanley's servant, lines 1–34); an enemy (Buckingham's spy, lines 35–71); another friend (Stanley, lines 72–95); two reminders of arrest and execution (the Pursuivant, the Priest, lines 96–112); and another enemy (Buckingham, lines 113–24).

Lines 1–34. Stanley's servant tells of his master's dream that the boar has torn off his helmet ('razèd off his helm'), revealing his fear that Richard will turn on Hastings and himself. The boar was Richard's emblem. Stanley also fears the 'two councils'. The 'real' council at Crosby Place will offer Richard the crown while a second, unimportant council will meet at the Tower to plan Prince Edward's coronation, which will never take place. Stanley believes they should escape now. Dreams carried great significance for Elizabethans, who would realise the foolishness of Hastings' response to such a powerful omen. Naively believing his 'good friend' Catesby, he is certain the 'boar will use us kindly' ('kindly' meaning not only 'in a caring way' but also the more sinister 'like a boar'). Hastings unwisely rebukes Stanley for believing in dreams.

Lines 35–71. The menace deepens as Catesby probes Hastings' intentions. 'Our tott'ring state' becomes 'a reeling world' as Catesby portrays a country drunk and out of control, with a crowned Richard the only solution. Hastings is ironically unaware that his reply predicts his fate: he will have his own 'crown' cut from his shoulders before seeing a crown 'so foul misplaced'. Hastings continues to parade his self-assurance, little understanding his references to the deaths of his enemies can also apply to himself. Catesby's replies are full of sinister implications and double meanings:

> 'Tis a vile thing to die, my gracious lord,
> When men are unprepared and look not for it.   *(lines 62–3)*

Lines 72–95. Hastings now feels 'triumphant' because he believes his future is secure. Stanley's warning that the imprisoned Rivers, Grey and Vaughan were happy ('jocund') when they rode to London to meet Prince Edward fails to shake Hastings' confidence. Stanley's warning of the fickleness of fate ('But yet you see how soon the day o'ercast') does not prevent him from accompanying Hastings to the Tower.

Some productions stress Hastings' celebrations at the downfall of his enemies by having him appear with his mistress, Jane Shore. Sometimes she appears at the opening of the scene as he dresses.

Some productions link Hastings' blind adoration for Mistress Shore to his inability to foresee his own danger.

Lines 96–112. Hastings fails to see the significance of his meetings with the Pursuivant (a royal messenger with the power to make arrests) who escorted him to the Tower, and a priest, whom he promises to pay on the following Sunday. Hastings mistakes them for symbols of his own freedom and future when they are in fact emblems of his approaching arrest and execution.

Lines 113–24. The reference to 'no shriving work' is both Buckingham's cruel joke, and is dramatically ironic. Buckingham's surface meaning is that Hastings is in no need of shriving (confession before death), but his aside reminds the audience that Hastings is doomed (he will stay for 'supper' – but he will be dead).

Act 3 Scene 3

Rivers, about to be executed, claims he will die for 'truth, for duty, and for loyalty'. He recalls the vicious cycle of death and retribution that began when Richard II was 'hacked to death' and Grey remembers Margaret's curses against them both 'For standing by when Richard stabbed her son.' Rivers comforts himself that Margaret's curses will visit Richard, Buckingham and Hastings, but also pleads with God to spare 'my sister and her princely sons'.

The Woodvilles' execution is the first in a number of formal, stylised and brief scenes where the victims of Richard's tyranny understand their place in the cycle of retribution. They realise the harsh realities associated with a deeply corrupt state ruled by a cruel despot as, like Clarence, they achieve a measure of self-knowledge the moment before their deaths. Their recall of Margaret's curses further reminds the audience of the future and the inevitable fate of Hastings, Buckingham and Richard.

Act 3 Scene 4

The council begin planning Prince Edward's coronation, unaware that their meeting is a sham, designed by Richard and Buckingham to engineer Hastings' downfall. Buckingham deceitfully denies his close association with Richard, arguing he knows Richard's outward appearance ('faces') but not his inward thoughts ('hearts'). In sharp contrast, foolish and over-confident Hastings claims a close relationship with Richard ('I know he loves me well.').

Survival in these dangerous times lies in the ability to correctly judge a person's real nature, and not be misled by external signs. Hastings will not survive because he demonstrates a fatal inability to distinguish between Richard's 'face' and 'heart'. He also fails to grasp the wider perspective: he is playing the role of foolish and trusting courtier assigned to him by two practised deceivers. Too late he will realise the foolishness of believing: 'For by his face straight shall you know his heart'.

Richard and Buckingham stage Hastings' downfall with chilling precision. Richard's opening words are deeply ironic as he expresses unconcern at the council's deliberations (because he knows there will be no coronation). Buckingham intensifies the drama by using theatrical metaphors ('cue', 'pronounced', 'part', 'your voice'). Richard's request for strawberries is purposefully contrived to delay the council and inform Buckingham that Hastings is against them. For contemporary audiences, strawberries were also richly symbolic, their external beauty symbolising earthly temptation and its attendant dangers.

Richard's second staged entrance is sudden, dramatic and forceful. He accuses Queen Elizabeth and 'strumpet' Shore of plotting his death through witchcraft. His arm ('like a blasted sapling, withered up') is proof of their treason. Hastings falls into the trap, guilty through association with Mistress Shore. Richard's order is brutal: 'Off with his head!'

Some admire Hastings' moral courage. The Lord Chancellor's unfaltering support of young Edward's claim to the throne reaffirms constitutional legitimacy. But Richard's ruthless and brutal manipulation of the political agenda renders Hastings friendless. His isolation is captured brilliantly in Olivier's film, as council members leave singly, each refusing to meet Hastings' eyes.

Hastings realises he has ignored or misinterpreted events and failed to respond to ominous signs. He accepts that Margaret's curse must now savagely come true. Hastings' image of the fragility of human nature like a drunken sailor on a mast echoes Clarence's dream about falling from the boat (Act 1 Scene 4, lines 16–20). Both realise too late that in pursuing earthly fame and ignoring the blessing of God they have failed to recognise the identity of their killer.

Act 3 Scene 5

Once again Shakespeare draws upon his theatrical experience to portray how Richard and Buckingham feign fear and terror in a brilliantly stage-managed scene to convince the Lord Mayor that Hastings had plotted against them and deserved execution without trial. Their malicious sense of fun aims to generate panic. Appearing in rusty, extremely ugly armour to win over the Lord Mayor, they will use identical techniques to those used by the actors of great tragedies in Shakespeare's time:

> Come, cousin, canst thou quake and change thy colour,
> Murder thy breath in middle of a word,
> And then again begin, and stop again,
> As if thou were distraught and mad with terror?   *(lines 1–4)*

They pretend they are under attack as they rush around the stage, frantically warding off imaginary enemies. In a supremely theatrical moment, Lovell and Ratcliffe dramatically reveal Hastings' severed head.

Richard and Buckingham manipulate the Lord Mayor with clever, deceiving words. Richard pretends he was tricked by the appearance of Hastings as 'the plainest harmless creature', but slyly mentions Hastings' sexual liaison with Jane Shore. Buckingham's revelation that Hastings was a secret traitor who plotted 'To murder me and my good lord of Gloucester' brings the Mayor's neutral response 'Had he done so?'

Richard's subtle invocation of Christian ethics, the law and the peace of England and the risk to their personal safety finally persuade the Lord Mayor. Richard is supported by Buckingham's flattering assurance that they both wanted the Mayor to witness Hastings' execution, but Lovell and Ratcliffe acted too impetuously. The Mayor leaves to tell the citizens Richard's version of events.

Critics note that Richard ironically adopts the role previously played by Hastings: an uncomplicated man who has foolishly failed to distinguish Hastings' harmless face from his false heart. The Lord Mayor becomes another of Richard's victims as he fails to distinguish the cruel reality behind the honest appearance.

Richard instructs Buckingham to spread rumours about Edward IV and his children, which question their legal right to claim the English throne. In the role of 'orator' at the Guildhall, Buckingham is to make four allegations to the Lord Mayor and leading citizens:

- That King Edward IV's children are illegitimate.
- That Edward ordered the unjust execution of a merchant who had told his son he would inherit his house, named 'The Crown'. Edward misinterpreted the merchant's wishes, believing he referred to his crown, meaning 'kingdom'.
- That Edward possessed a lustful nature.
- That King Edward himself was illegitimate, because the Duchess of York conceived him while her husband was fighting in France, and there is no physical resemblance between father and son.

The two plotters will meet at 'three or four o'clock' to continue their charade at Baynard's Castle. Buckingham will continue in the role of 'orator' and supporting actors will include 'reverend fathers and well-learnèd bishops'.

Act 3 Scene 6

In a soliloquy the Scrivener (a professional scribe who drafts legal documents) reflects on the deceit involved in Hastings' execution. He estimates Hastings was charged five hours before the original accusation and questions whether there is a person so stupid ('gross') who cannot see such obvious trickery. He comments that Richard is creating a world where people are afraid of criticising obvious injustice. The Scrivener's fourteen lines are in sonnet form but without the rhymes, except for the final couplet. They reflect his learned disposition and add credibility to his accusations. The scene ironically recalls Prince Edward's reflections on the importance of 'registered' records: 'Methinks the truth should live from age to age' (Act 3 Scene 1, line 76). Hastings' indictment is a false document that could be used by future historians to make the illegal appear legitimate.

The scene (like Act 2 Scene 3) portrays the powerlessness of ordinary subjects, whose private fears dare not be voiced publicly in a corrupt state. The concerns of the Three Citizens and the Scrivener come to represent the general fear of all subjects. They anticipate the reluctance of the citizens to be convinced by Richard and Buckingham in the next scene.

Act 3 Scene 7

The Scrivener's scene has allowed time for Buckingham to make his speech to the citizens. He now tells of his frosty reception at the Guildhall. The citizens remained silent as he slandered Edward and praised Richard. He has used the four allegations suggested by Richard and added more of his own:

- The rumour that Edward had been engaged to Elizabeth Lucy.
- The rumour that Edward dishonoured a deputy (negotiator) who had arranged for him to marry the sister-in-law of the king of France.
- Richard was indeed a brave war leader, who captured the Scottish city of Berwick in 1482, but Buckingham falsely adds 'virtue, fair humility'.

Buckingham's oratory is not successful. He has complicated already difficult issues by embellishing Richard's original rumours and has ignored protocol by addressing the citizens directly rather than following the established procedure of allowing the Recorder to speak to the people. His comment 'No, so God help me, they spake not a word' often gets a laugh in the theatre. Buckingham is an astute politician and skilled spin-doctor. He reclaims some dignity by contriving that ten of his followers cry 'God save King Richard!' after the Recorder's farcical repetition of the allegations. He ensures that the final scene of the travesty is enacted not at the Guildhall, but in the theatrical setting of Richard's family home of Baynard's Castle (its balconies resembling an Elizabethan playhouse) where Buckingham will beg reluctant Richard to accept the crown.

Buckingham jokes on the proverb which states that virgins say 'no' to sexual advances when they mean 'yes' and Richard hopes his 'nay' will bring a successful birth. Their sexual banter stands in sharp contrast to Buckingham's instruction to Richard to appear saintly before the Mayor. But Richard's 'nay' also ironically foreshadows his refusal to grant Buckingham the promised Earldom of Hereford (Act 4 Scene 2).

Buckingham and Catesby prepare the Mayor and citizens for Richard's fearful and pious entrance. Catesby's words stress Richard's unworldly nature: 'meditation', 'reverend fathers', 'Divinely' and 'holy exercise'. Buckingham keeps his promise and plays a variety of ingenious variations ('descant') on Richard's repeated theme ('ground') of pretended piety. In a series of graphic contrasts, he compares pious Richard with lascivious Edward. Catesby even reports that Richard fears the citizens will harm him: 'He fears, my lord, you mean no good to him.'

Richard appears on a balcony between two bishops, reading a book of prayer. It is one of the great comic and dramatic moments of the play. Richard delights in his role of mock piety, but many in the Elizabethan audience would be horrified by the sacrilegious image. Ridiculing religion and divine law, Richard has set himself against God in his quest for the crown (see page 64).

Buckingham also puts on a performance to deceive the Lord Mayor. In a brilliant display of rhetoric he appeals to Richard's patriotism and ignores his personal ambition:

- Buckingham tells Richard he is wrong to give up his right to the crown in favour of corrupt members of his family.
- He urges Richard to awake to action because England is sick and her royal family at the point of death.
- The people beg Richard to cure England by becoming not an agent of another, but the true king, in his own right.
- He claims that all this is the wish of the citizens.

Richard continues his deceitful acting. He rejects Buckingham's offer of the crown. He too uses formal language that claims to be a struggle to conceal his true thoughts. He debates whether to be silent or to speak. His silence might be interpreted as acceptance of the crown; if he speaks it may seem like a reprimand to good friends. But even in his false humility Richard makes the distinction between his high 'degree' (he is also literally above them) and the lower 'condition' of the citizens. Richard argues he is not fit to be monarch. He compares himself to a ship unfit to endure a great ocean, arguing he would rather avoid kingship than desire it and be overwhelmed by such an awesome responsibility. But 'ripe revenue', 'due of birth', and the repetition of 'me' and 'my' reveals he is claiming the throne even as he appears to reject it. He asserts the Prince of Wales is the rightful heir, who will mature into a distinguished monarch. But his 'no doubt' is a sting in the tail of his praise of Edward:

The royal tree hath left us royal fruit,
Which, mellowed by the stealing hours of time,

Will well become the seat of majesty
And make (no doubt) us happy by his reign.   *(lines 166–9)*

Buckingham's reply repeats accusations against Prince Edward and King Edward and adds new insults against Elizabeth. This is the third occasion when the Lord Mayor and citizens have listened to slanderous rumour. The Lord Mayor is either convinced by the arguments or so wearied by their repetition that he adds his (probably) sincere voice to the deeply insincere voices of Catesby and Buckingham. All beg Richard to become their king, but Richard enjoys the danger of taking his performance to the brink and refuses the kingship.

On film, Olivier veered dangerously out of control as Richard. He played up to Buckingham's description of his virtues ('tenderness', 'gentle', 'kind') and dropped his prayer book in horror when Buckingham stated 'But we will plant some other in the throne'. Some stage productions make a long pause after Buckingham's exit so Richard is genuinely afraid they will not return. His 'Call them again' has a note of genuine panic that often creates audience laughter.

Richard finally accepts the crown in a hypocritical speech of great cunning. He must patiently accept the burden of kingship that is fastened like armour on his malformed back. He shifts responsibility away from himself and onto those who imposed kingship on him. Repetition of the pronouns 'I', 'you', 'your' and words meaning 'burden' and 'fault' reinforce his appearance of grudging acceptance:

Since you will buckle fortune on my back,
To bear her burden, whe'er I will or no,
I must have patience to endure the load.   *(lines 226–8)*

Many productions end the scene with a striking image as a triumphant Richard is proclaimed king. In one stage production Richard threw away his prayer book and the bishops revealed themselves as armed soldiers. In Olivier's film, Richard's final action was to force Buckingham to kneel and kiss his hand in an act of submission.

Act 3: Critical review

Act 3 contains the most scenes and largest number of locations in the play as it portrays Richard's wide-ranging and successful plans to become king. He defies the Church, imprisons the rightful heir to the throne, executes four influential nobles who oppose him, and cynically manipulates the Lord Mayor and citizens.

Richard advances his plans by acting out a variety of roles. His appearances as caring uncle, victim of witchcraft, pious worshipper and reluctant king imbue many episodes with mocking humour that frequently masks his evil intentions. His flamboyant role-play creates a variety of contrasting language: rhetorical in the council and with the citizens; witty wordplay in his exchanges with York and Buckingham; dismissive and full of dramatic irony with Hastings; theatrical as he and Buckingham fool the Lord Mayor.

The menacing Tower of London continues to dominate as a potent symbol of repression throughout the act. In an episode of great pathos, the two young princes are escorted into it. Hastings is advised not to attend the council meeting. When he foolishly ignores dreams and omens, the Tower becomes his grave. Another bloody symbol of despotism, Pomfret Castle, is the location for the executions of Grey, Rivers and Vaughan. All the executions reinforce Richard's inexorable march towards power.

Richard's dependence upon Buckingham to carry out his plans continues to the end of the act. Buckingham reveals his talents as organiser and orator, but he is no Richard. He fails initially to persuade the citizens to accept Richard as king and overcomplicates Richard's instructions. But the two arch-deceivers generate much of the mocking humour and grotesque comedy that is such a feature of the act as they clown their way to power.

The end of the act marks the climax of Richard's ambition. But in the midst of his triumph there are ominous signs. The Three Citizens' views, related in the previous act, anticipate the unenthusiastic reception given by the citizens of London. The Scrivener reveals duplicity at the highest level, but he is powerless. Most ominously of all for Richard, the audience is reminded of Margaret's curse and the inevitable cycle of revenge that will only end in Richard's death.

Act 4 Scene 1

The opening of Act 4 focuses on the victims of Richard's newly acquired power, as members of the late King Edward's family attempt to visit the princes in the Tower. The three females stress their close family ties ('niece Plantagenet', 'aunt', 'Daughter' and 'sister') as they unite in their adversity. Brakenbury bars their way, obeying Richard's orders that the princes must be isolated (Act 3 Scene 5, lines 108–9). Nothing the women say can persuade Brakenbury to relent.

Stanley's news that Richard is to be crowned 'one hour hence' horrifies everyone. Elizabeth quickly realises the danger to her family and is pragmatic and decisive. She urges Dorset (her son) to leave the country and join the Earl of Richmond in France. Elizabeth recalls Margaret's curse (Act 1 Scene 3, line 207): she is no longer wife or queen, but she will die a mother if Dorset escapes. Stanley will provide letters to his stepson Richmond to speed Dorset's escape.

The three women express their intense hatred of Richard in powerful images. Elizabeth says Dorset must escape an England that has become a 'hell' and 'slaughterhouse'. The Duchess laments her 'accursèd womb' as a 'bed of death' that has given birth to a 'cockatrice' (a monster, believed to kill by its look). Anne wishes the crown were 'red-hot steel' and the coronation oil a 'deadly venom' so she can die before she is proclaimed Richard's queen. She recalls Richard's wooing and her curse on him (Act 1 Scene 2, lines 14–28) that has become a curse upon herself. With Richard absent, those closest to him have reminded the audience of his evil nature.

Critics point to parallels between this scene and Resurrection plays: the earliest morality plays that re-enacted Jesus' rising from the dead (see page 66). In the central episode, three women approach Jesus' tomb and rejoice when told by angels that their Lord has risen. This scene inverts that re-creation of Christian celebration and salvation. Three women approach the Tower to lament the imprisonment of the princes who will not be saved. Elizabeth's fruitless plea for the Tower to show pity on the two princes contrasts the impersonal, menacing prison with the vulnerable, innocent boys:

> Rude, ragged nurse, old sullen playfellow
> For tender princes, use my babies well.   *(lines 102–3)*

Act 4 Scene 2

Richard, now the crowned king, sits on the throne. It represents the moment he has craved for so long. Victorian productions often staged Richard's entrance with pomp and splendour, but modern directors frequently expose Richard as an unworthy king. Antony Sher revealed Richard's deformity by stripping to the waist before slithering, snake-like, onto a chair. In another production a tiny Richard sat on an enormous throne that dwarfed him. But Richard fears losing the crown at the very moment he possesses it:

> But shall we wear these glories for a day?
> Or shall they last, and we rejoice in them?   *(lines 6–7)*

Richard tests Buckingham's loyalty by first insinuating, then explicitly stating his desire for the princes' deaths: 'I wish the bastards dead'. Buckingham does not give Richard the answer he wants. He is 'ice' and his 'kindness freezes' as he asks for time to consider.

Catesby's remark 'The king is angry; see, he gnaws his lip' exposes Richard's true state of mind to other characters for perhaps the first time in the play. Once again, he shares his thoughts with the audience, but now the glee of Act 1 is replaced with bitter disillusion. He will surround himself with stupid and unfeeling persons, and he contemptuously dismisses 'High-reaching Buckingham'.

Stanley's news that Dorset has joined Richmond prompts Richard to a torrent of malign plots. Putting his plans into instant action, he sends for the corrupt Tyrrel. He will marry Clarence's daughter to a 'poor gentleman'; let Clarence's son live (he is no threat because he is mentally ill); kill the princes in the Tower; bring about Anne's death and then marry Edward IV's daughter, Elizabeth. Richard's brutality was captured memorably in the Royal Shakespeare Company production of 1992. Anne was on stage, throned alongside Richard. He leant across her while repeating his instructions for her death warrant to a shocked Catesby: 'Anne my queen is sick and like to die.'

Richard's rapid, even frantic, decisions were used by Jan Kott (see page 93) to support his argument that a history play becomes tragedy the moment a king realises he has ascended the throne only to be toppled from power. Richard realises 'my kingdom stands on brittle glass' and acknowledges his profound guilt, for he is 'So far in blood that sin will pluck on sin'. Wolfgang Clemens writes 'one is conscious [in this scene] of the approaching catastrophe. The rise must be followed by the fall'.

The final episodes of the scene contrast the rise of Tyrrel with the fall of Buckingham. Tyrrel is to kill 'those bastards in the Tower' and claim a reward. On film, Olivier as Richard added to the horror by issuing his orders from behind a pillow, anticipating the princes' suffocation. Tyrrel's ready agreement shows that Richard's brutal regime demands unquestioning loyalty, not shared cunning. Buckingham discovers that harsh fact when he claims the title and wealth that Richard promised him, and is bluntly refused:

BUCKINGHAM   May it please you to resolve me in my suit?
RICHARD   Thou troublest me; I am not in the vein.   *(lines 100–1)*

Buckingham resolves to flee to the safety of Wales.

Act 4 Scene 3

Tyrrel has carried out Richard's orders. Now he describes the profound remorse of Dighton and Forrest, who smothered the princes. His emotionally charged soliloquy, with its calculated poetic language stressing the vulnerability of the princes, deliberately evokes pathos. The murder is

> The most arch deed of piteous massacre
> That ever yet this land was guilty of.   *(lines 2–3)*

The hardened murderers were moved to tears at the 'gentle babes'. They almost changed their minds when they saw 'a book of prayers' on the princes' pillow. This visual reminder of the Christian faith afflicts Dighton and Forrest with 'conscience and remorse'. Traditional stagings underlined the pity and horror of the murder. Modern productions, concerned to emphasise the inhumanity of Richard's regime, often portray Tyrrel full of contempt as he cynically describes Dighton and Forrest's sensitivity and 'conscience'. Tyrrel briefly assures Richard that the princes are dead and the bodies buried.

Elizabethan audiences would associate Richard's evil act with the tyrant Herod. In medieval mystery plays he was the biblical figure responsible for the slaughter of all male babies born in his kingdom (referred to as 'The Massacre of the Innocents') at the time of the birth of Jesus (see page 66).

Richard's soliloquy lists the successes he has achieved: Clarence's son imprisoned, his daughter married to a nonentity, the princes murdered, Anne dead. Some critics argue that Richard lacks his previous charisma and lethal charm after he becomes king, and that here he uses the audience for self-assurance. Others believe the audacious, witty and self-mocking Richard of old cannot be suppressed. He appears to be his gleefully wicked self as he plans to marry young Elizabeth to strengthen his hold on the throne: 'To her go I, a jolly thriving wooer.' But Ratcliffe brings bad news. Richard's enemies are closing in. Richard opts for immediate military action:

> Then fiery expedition be my wing,
> Jove's Mercury, and herald for a king!   *(lines 54–5)*

Act 4 Scene 4
The scene contains four episodes:

- Three women united in grief (lines 1–135).
- Richard's encounter with his mother (lines 136–96).
- Richard's encounter with Elizabeth (lines 197–436).
- Military matters (lines 437–547).

Lines 1–135. Three women from rival factions – Queen Margaret (Lancaster), the Duchess (York) and Elizabeth (Woodville) – unite in lamentation and curse Richard. Each woman's contribution to the dialogue is now examined in turn.

Queen Margaret. Hiding within the walls of the court, vengeful Margaret has watched the loss of power ('waning') of the Yorkists and Woodvilles. Her opening words ironically recall Richard's opening soliloquy: now the 'glorious summer' of Yorkist supremacy has decayed into the autumnal rot of Richard's reign. Margaret also echoes Richard's theatrical imagery ('induction', 'consequence', 'tragical') as she hopes for further disasters. Margaret has watched her enemies' downfall and hopes that Richard's new cycle of murder will have tragic consequences.

As Elizabeth and the Duchess mourn, Margaret's asides show she views each death as justice or repayment for her own losses ('right for right', 'doth quit', 'pays a dying debt'). In formal, ritualistic language she joins the Duchess in mourning fourteen deaths, but blames the Duchess for giving birth to 'hell-hound' Richard. She claims the devil keeps Richard alive as a spy and agent to send others to hell, and she prays he will soon die and go to hell himself. In a long and highly patterned speech Margaret recalls her descriptions of Elizabeth and contrasts Elizabeth's past happiness when queen with her present miserable condition. Margaret's final act before she leaves for France is to teach the two remaining women how to curse.

Elizabeth grieves for her two sons, murdered in the Tower. She questions why God has allowed her sons to be killed by 'the wolf' Richard. Recalling Margaret's prophecy that she would ask her help to curse Richard ('That bottled spider, that foul bunch-backed toad'), Elizabeth finally asks Margaret to teach her how to curse.

The Duchess of York mourns for King Edward. She describes herself, using three oxymorons ('Dead life, blind sight', 'living ghost'); as a stage where griefs are acted out ('Woe's scene'); as the shame of the world (because she gave birth to Richard); and as someone who has lived too long. She joins Margaret in ritualistically listing all the deaths and tells Elizabeth to complain bitterly and often to Richard.

Traditional criticism of 'the wailing women' attributed the serious tone and formal, balanced structure of the language to the influence of Seneca (see page 64). Other critics have interpreted *King Richard III* as the embodiment of the Tudor myth (see pages 58 and 90), believing that the purpose of the play was to portray the working out of God's will in English history. Tillyard (the best-known critic who supported this interpretation) portrayed the women as observers and commentators, powerless to influence God's pre-ordained plan. He defines their lamentations as reflecting the piety of the Middle Ages: 'ritual, incantory and ecclesiastical' in tone. A P Rossiter disagrees and sees them as a 'dismal catalogue of Who was Who and Who has lost Whom'. Nonetheless, Rossiter admires the stylised nature of the patterned speech and notes how it parallels the carefully patterned structure of the play. More recently, feminist criticism has celebrated the women speaking as equals and supporting each other in an overtly masculine play (see page 97). Their courageous choric voice is a significant contribution to Richard's downfall.

Lines 136–96. The Duchess and Elizabeth intercept Richard's military expedition to defeat Buckingham. Both women assault Richard with the only weapons they possess – words. Margaret has taught them how to curse, and now they trumpet Richard's evil nature and terrible crimes. Their public condemnation echoes what the Three Citizens (Act 2 Scene 3) and the Scrivener (Act 3 Scene 6) have privately expressed.

The Duchess says she should have strangled Richard 'in her accursèd womb'. She twice calls him 'toad' as she accuses him of murdering his brother. Elizabeth accuses Richard of murdering her relatives to inherit the crown. How does Richard react? Stage productions sometimes portray an infantile Richard, banging a drum to avoid hearing such terrible truths.

The Duchess chillingly rejects her son as she recalls his life with a litany of adjectives that made 'the earth my hell':

> A grievous burden was thy birth to me.
> Tetchy and wayward was thy infancy;
> Thy schooldays frightful, desperate, wild, and furious;
> Thy prime of manhood, daring, bold, and venturous;
> Thy age confirmed, proud, subtle, sly, and bloody
>
> *(lines 168–72)*

Her parting words are a prophecy and curse. Richard will be justly killed by God's decree before the war is over, or she will die. She will pray for the opposing side, and predicts the souls of the murdered princes will promise victory to Richmond. Her final rhyming couplet wishes for Richard's death in battle, and personifies 'Shame' as a servant following Richard in life and waiting for him in death:

> Bloody thou art, bloody will be thy end;
> Shame serves thy life and doth thy death attend.
>
> *(lines 195–6)*

Lines 197–436. In this episode, Richard attempts to woo young Princess Elizabeth through her mother. Richard anticipates success, but Elizabeth proves a worthy adversary. The episode begins with Elizabeth anticipating Richard's wishes and protecting her daughters, who 'shall be praying nuns, not weeping queens'. Feminist critics argue this powerful opening statement reveals that Elizabeth wants her daughters, not the men in the play, to have control over their own bodies.

Elizabeth will do anything to save her daughter from Richard. She ironically uses the vicious rumours Richard had spread about the illegitimacy of her children to save young Elizabeth ('Slander myself as false to Edward's bed'), for Richard must marry a legitimate daughter to preserve his kingship. Elizabeth describes the murder of her two sons ('my lambs') as a sacrifice, and in an extended nautical metaphor wishes she could die attacking Richard:

> Till that my nails were anchored in thine eyes,
> And I in such a desperate bay of death,
> Like a poor bark of sails and tackling reft,
> Rush all to pieces on thy rocky bosom.   *(lines 232–5)*

Elizabeth argues he can only offer her family more death, but Richard protests he will banish her grief by giving all honour and dignity to her daughter ('Even all I have'). Richard wishes to marry Elizabeth's daughter and make her queen of England. He asks for Elizabeth's help as a mother who best knows her daughter's mood and character. Elizabeth's mocking reply challenges Richard to send her daughter the results of his murderous deeds as grisly gifts ('A pair of bleeding hearts'). Richard repeats the argument that proved so effective when he wooed Anne 'Say that I did all this for love of her' but Elizabeth is unmoved, for her daughter 'cannot choose but hate thee'.

Richard's reply ('Men shall deal unadvisedly sometimes') usually gains a big laugh in the theatre because 'deal unadvisedly' is totally out of proportion to the enormity of his crimes. But Richard is unabashed. He lists the gains Elizabeth will enjoy as the future queen mother. In his long speech (lines 295–340), Richard makes over 20 references to family: daughter (five); mother (three); children (two); son/s (three); Dorset (two). He also refers to 'wife', 'grandam', 'blood', birth, 'wife'. But in urging the paramount importance of family life, he ironically champions the very institution he has destroyed. His appeal to kinship is persuasive but the words carry chilling implications:

> If I have killed the issue of your womb,
> To quicken your increase I will beget
> Mine issue of your blood upon your daughter.   *(lines 300–2)*

Richard argues the advantages to Elizabeth as a grandmother (lines 303–40). Her son might not be king, but her daughter will be queen. Dorset can return home to a position of power. Elizabeth's past troubles will be resolved as mother to the queen and her future will be happier. Elizabeth must use her maturity to prepare her daughter for wooing, queenship and the joys of marriage. Richard concludes by promising that when he has defeated Buckingham he will marry young Elizabeth and she will be his commander.

Elizabeth responds with a series of questions to Richard's proposal (lines 341–6) as she mockingly asks 'Under what title shall I woo for thee . . .?' What follows as Elizabeth counters Richard's arguments (lines 347–71) is a quickfire exchange of *stichomythia* (see page 76) often using balanced, antithetical pairing of sentences. It mirrors a similar exchange with Anne (Act 1 Scene 2). In this back-and-forth exchange, Elizabeth accuses Richard of disregarding three basic principles that govern a stable society ('God', 'law', 'honour'). Taking up her challenge, Richard searches for a symbol by which he may swear an oath so Elizabeth will believe him. He attempts to swear on the symbols of kingship, but Elizabeth shows he has 'profaned', 'blemished', and 'usurped' each. He attempts to swear an oath based on himself, the world, his father's death, heaven, the future. His final answer is dismissed with contempt by Elizabeth (lines 393–401) for the future will be filled with children grieving for their parents and parents for their children that Richard has killed.

Richard's final argument to Elizabeth is the strongest – the state will collapse without this marriage alliance (lines 402–22). Richard paints a picture of the country ruined ('Death, desolation, ruin, and decay') if Princess Elizabeth will not marry him. Elizabeth replies with a rhetorical question that recalls her earlier accusations that he is the devil, and she reminds Richard that he murdered her children. Richard's response is breathtaking:

> But in your daughter's womb I bury them,
> Where in that nest of spicery they will breed
> Selves of themselves, to your recomforture. *(lines 428–30)*

Richard's image is that of the mythical phoenix. Just as the phoenix dies in flames by burning its nest to be reborn in the ashes ('nest of spicery') so new children will be reborn from Richard's dead victims to console ('recomforture') Elizabeth. The phoenix image traditionally represented spiritual renewal and rebirth. Richard seems to believe he can begin afresh by fathering new children from the ashes of those he has murdered. Psychoanalytic critics (see page 103) argue the image reveals Richard's unconscious desire to be mothered by Elizabeth (he twice calls her 'mother' in the scene) after his rejection by the Duchess. Others assert that the image is repulsive but erotic, and betrays Richard's disgust with women and breeding. His encounters with the women in the scene have lost him a mother's support and hopes for dynastic succession, but for the moment he believes he has won: 'Relenting fool and shallow, changing woman.'

Is Elizabeth persuaded? A few productions suggest that Elizabeth is willing to woo her daughter on Richard's behalf. But most interpretations show her as fooling Richard by persuading her daughter not to marry him.

Critics identify parallels with his wooing of Anne (Act 1 Scene 2). Both episodes are expressed in formal, often stylised language that uses repetition and antithesis, and both episodes form part of the larger structure of the play (see page 81). The successful wooing of Anne balances the attempted wooing of young Elizabeth. Richard's earlier success with Anne reflected his mesmerising power and growing success at that point in the play; his endeavour to convince Elizabeth signals those powers weakening.

Lines 437–547. Three short sequences expose Richard's deteriorating position and growing insecurity: he gives confused orders to Catesby and Ratcliffe; shows distrust of Stanley; and reacts illogically to messengers' reports.

Ratcliffe brings news of Richmond's threatened invasion and of unreliable allies ('hollow-hearted friends'). Richard's orders are confused. He instructs Catesby to 'fly to the duke' (of Norfolk) but forgets to give him the message. Within moments of commanding Ratcliffe to precede him to the city of Salisbury, Richard cannot remember the reason for his order, and reverses it.

Stanley reports that Richmond is about to invade. Supported by Dorset, Buckingham and Morton (the Bishop of Ely), he comes to claim the throne. Richard's response 'Is the chair empty?' can be a great dramatic moment. On film, Olivier screamed the line as he rushed to the throne to be reassured of his ownership.

Richard is suspicious of Stanley's loyalty. He forecasts that Stanley will change sides and help Richmond ('the Welshman') when he arrives in Wales. Stanley claims to be loyal and says he will raise an army to join Richard. Still distrusting Stanley, Richard insists that Stanley's son, George, be left as a hostage, to be killed if Stanley proves disloyal.

Four messengers and Catesby report growing unrest, rebellion and invasion. The first two messengers bring Richard unwelcome news of increasing support for Buckingham in Devonshire and Kent. The third messenger reports that Buckingham's army is scattered and Buckingham has been declared a traitor. The fourth messenger brings bad news that Yorkshire is in rebellion, but also the good news that Richmond's army is dispersed. Catesby reports that Buckingham has been captured, but Richmond has 'with a mighty power' landed at Milford Haven on the Welsh coast.

In this final episode, Shakespeare condenses two years of history. The events actually took place between October 1483 (Richmond's first attempt to land in England) and August 1485 (just before the Battle of Bosworth Field). Shakespeare's compression increases the dramatic effect. It conveys Richard's rapidly weakening position and shows his impulsive reactions to the contradictory reports: confused orders; changes of mind; striking a messenger; hasty decisions taken without advice. All suggest a character under great stress, but his final words seem full of determination:

> Away towards Salisbury! While we reason here
> A royal battle might be won and lost. *(lines 544–5)*

Act 4 Scene 5

Shakespeare uses this scene to show that Stanley's true loyalties are to Richmond, and to reveal that Elizabeth has deceived Richard: she has already agreed to her daughter marrying Richmond. But Stanley cannot reveal his true loyalty is to Richmond (Stanley is Richmond's stepfather). With his son held hostage 'in the sty of the most deadly boar' he cannot openly support Richmond.

Sir Christopher Urswick (a priest to the Countess of Richmond, Stanley's third wife) reveals the increasing power of Richard's enemies as he lists all those 'of great name and worth' that have joined forces with Richmond and marched to London.

Act 4: Critical review

The act marks the beginning of Richard's decline in fortune. In the first scene, events are portrayed at a rapid pace as news of Richard's impending coronation provokes the first signs of opposition. Queen Elizabeth and the Duchess of York collaborate with Stanley and Richmond to ensure Dorset's escape to France. Opposition to Richard gathers strength as Buckingham and then Ely desert. Richmond lands with an army, and important nobles join him.

Richard loses much of his lethal charm and sureness of touch as forces gather against him. Surrounding himself with vicious murderers (Tyrrel, Catesby and Ratcliffe) Richard gives confused orders, changes his mind, makes hasty decisions and strikes a messenger. But he has his successes: Clarence's children are rendered harmless; Edward's children murdered; his wife dies. For a moment he is his wicked self as he plans to marry young Elizabeth and tighten his grip on the crown.

The longest scene in the play focuses on the women who are united in their hatred of Richard. As each laments the death of loved ones in formal, ritualistic language, they remind the audience of Richard's true nature and his part in the cycle of murder and revenge. Before she leaves for France, Margaret passes her power of cursing to the Duchess of York and Queen Elizabeth. The inheritors of Margaret's powers, the two women will use their new-found mastery over words to expose Richard and his crimes.

That exposure begins immediately, and Richard loses a war of words not once, but twice. The Duchess reviles Richard, visiting him with a mother's curse and wishing for his death. Richard has no answer, and he orders his drummers to drown the Duchess' words. Richard then fails to convince Queen Elizabeth in his attempt to marry young Elizabeth. He has been publicly humiliated by his mother and outsmarted by the politically astute Elizabeth.

Richard's lethal humour and love of role-play was an essential feature of the first three acts. Act 4 provides a contrast by dramatically revealing the effects of Richard's evil schemes. The act brings together almost all those who have suffered from Richard's cruel plots and the effects of *realpolitik* are exposed.

Act 5 Scene 1

Escorted to his execution, Buckingham begs that if the souls of Richard's victims are watching him now, they should mock him. All Souls' Day (November 2) is appropriate for Buckingham's plea as it is the day in the Christian calendar when the living are especially encouraged to remember the dead. Some critics argue that November also fits the pattern of seasonal imagery begun by Richard in his opening soliloquy and renewed by Margaret (Act 4 Scene 4), signifying Richard is in the late autumn of his reign.

Buckingham acknowledges he has joked ('dallied') with God by swearing false loyalty to King Edward and is now punished by God (Act 2 Scene 1, lines 32–40). He reflects on how he dismissed Margaret's warning about Richard's real nature (Act 1 Scene 3, lines 289–94) and goes to execution accepting he deserves death.

Act 5 Scene 2

Richmond's troops have marched unopposed into central England. He now motivates them for battle. He portrays Richard as a 'usurping boar' which has overthrown the rightful king, and now kills and feasts on his own people as he ravages England. Richard has plundered ('spoiled') the land, but Richmond will 'reap the harvest of perpetual peace'. Richmond's words stress peace, hope and trust in God. The actor Antony Sher describes him as 'a breath of fresh air after hours of murder, mayhem and misery'.

Act 5 Scene 3

The scene portrays events from sunset to early morning. The action alternates between the rival camps of Richard and Richmond as the two leaders reflect upon their personal situations and prepare for the coming battle. The alternating episodes enable the audience to make direct comparisons and contrasts between the opposing sides.

Richard prepares for battle. Lines 1–18. Richard's customary self-confidence appears to desert him 'Here will I lie tonight, / But where tomorrow?'; however, he takes comfort in his superior number of soldiers. He enquires why Surrey looks 'so sad' and acknowledges the wounds and bloodshed to come ('must have knocks'). He boasts that 'the king's name is a tower of strength', but the words ignore his true position as usurper and tyrant.

Richmond gives orders. Lines 19–47. Richmond interprets the promise of fair weather ('a goodly day tomorrow') as an optimistic omen for the next day's battle, perhaps suggesting that the sky will shine on him but frown on Richard. He is courteous to those under his command, calling Blunt 'good' and 'Sweet' on the four occasions he addresses him. Blunt willingly agrees to risk his life in taking a message to Stanley ('Upon my life') and he invokes God to give Richmond 'quiet rest tonight'.

Further preparations for battle. Lines 48–81. Richard's short sentences and rapid changes of subject reveal his unsettled state of mind. Norfolk must choose 'trusty' guards. Stanley's son will be killed if Stanley does not bring troops to him. Richard's heartless pun ('sunrising' and 'son George fall') is a sharp reminder of his cruelty compared to Richmond's humanity. Richard's chilling lines on George Stanley's future ('Into the blind cave of eternal night') anticipates Richard's own approaching night of terror. Richard reflects that he has lost his cheerfulness of mind ('alacrity of spirit') and he twice demands a bowl of wine. As he settles to sleep, his repeated order 'Leave me' to Ratcliffe and Catesby seems to stress his isolation.

Richmond meets Stanley. Lines 82–120. Stanley's genuine affection for his stepson ('bless thee', 'vows of love', 'friends' and 'rites of love') contrasts vividly with his earlier guarded responses to Richard's request for assistance (Act 4 Scene 4, lines 463–505). Stanley acts as a catalyst to reveal the differences between Richard and Richmond. Both commanders need his support, but while family ties unite Richmond and Stanley, Richard holds George Stanley hostage and threatens his death. McKellen's film portrays George as the most helpless of all Richard's intended victims, a very small boy with thick glasses.

Richmond's prayer asks God to bless his army 'Look on my forces with a gracious eye' and support them as they fight against Richard. The army will then be 'ministers of chastisement' and it will be God's victory that is celebrated.

The ghosts of Richard's victims visit the two sleeping leaders. Lines 121–79. The Duchess of York's curse on her son (Act 4 Scene 4, lines 188–94) has come true. Appearing in the order of their deaths, Richard's eleven victims nine times condemn him to 'Despair and die' and offer

Richmond victory and success ('Live and flourish', 'pray', 'win', 'conquer').

Richard's bloody deeds are compressed into a succession of brief, nightmarish appearances that force him, through his dreams, to realise the enormity of his crimes. Richard knows he is a sinner, yet he cannot repent. 'Despair' is the ultimate Christian sin. It implies that Richard has put himself beyond the reach of God's forgiveness, and his soul will be forever damned (see page 62). The ghosts' formal language of repetition, balance and contrast reflects the language of the pageant or morality play (see page 65). The stylised presentation, with its roots in early religious drama, implies that Richard's real opponent is God, not Richmond.

Michael Bogdanov's 1987 production gave each ghost recognisable gestures to individualise them (for example, Clarence drinks wine, Anne spits). In another production, the ghosts did not appear to the dreaming commanders in their tents, but at the Battle of Bosworth. They took part in the action and wounded Richard in the fighting. This staging suggests that although Richmond physically killed Richard in a real sword fight, it was from psychological rather than physical wounds that he died.

Richard starts from the nightmare. Lines 180–209. Richard's agonised soliloquy attempts to come to terms with the 'several sins' that weigh on his conscience. His opening words 'Give me another horse!' anticipate his anguished final line in the play (Act 5 Scene 4, line 13). He prays for mercy 'Have mercy, Jesu!' but as he returns to wakefulness he immediately ceases his pleas for forgiveness 'Soft, I did but dream.' Richard's conscience forces him to recognise the consequences of his actions ('Perjury' and 'Murder') that now proclaim his guilt to all ('Guilty, guilty!'). He almost gives in to the despair first urged on him by Anne (Act 1 Scene 2, lines 86–8) and now by the ghosts ('I shall despair'). He is forced to recognise the horror of exclusion from earthly and heavenly love and pity ('There is no creature loves me') and he wonders how others can love him when he finds no pity within himself.

Richard reflects on his inner confusion in over 30 brief sentences as he jumps from thought to thought, mood to mood. For many, this passage represents Richard's principal conflict. His mental struggle against God and his conscience represents a greater battle than the physical one against Richmond at Bosworth. Some claim Richard's troubled soliloquy heralds the beginnings of modern psychological drama, giving direct insight into a character's innermost thoughts.

Richard admits his fear. Lines 210–23. Ratcliffe reminds Richard it is dawn and urges him not to fear 'shadows'. Richard says 'shadows' (delusions or ghosts) have struck more terror into his soul than 10,000 soldiers. Richard had earlier spoken of his hatred of the sun and his preference for shadows (Act 1 Scene 1, lines 24–7). Now those shadows return to terrify him.

Richmond motivates his soldiers. Lines 224–71. While Richard has suffered nightmares, Richmond has enjoyed a peaceful night ('The sweetest sleep and fairest-boding dreams'). He tells his army that God and right are on their side. Regretting that he has little time for his oration, he:

- assures the soldiers that God is on their side and that they are fighting for a just cause;
- claims that all Richard's followers want Richmond to win because they know Richard is a usurper and not a true king;
- again reminds his soldiers that God is on their side, and lists the advantages for the future that will be gained by fighting now;
- declares that if he succeeds the soldiers will all share his victory;
- ends with a rallying cry:

> Sound drums and trumpets boldly and cheerfully.
> God and Saint George, Richmond and victory!   *(lines 270–1)*

Richard prepares for battle. Lines 272–353. Richard and Ratcliffe have eavesdropped on conversations but failed to find treachery. Now Richard interprets the sun rising an hour late as a bad omen for someone, and then dismisses it as of no significance 'For the self-same heaven / That frowns on me looks sadly upon him.' Shakespeare uses both time and the weather dramatically and symbolically throughout the scene to contrast Richmond's success with Richard's failure. Richard, in his opening soliloquy in Act 1, spoke of 'all the clouds that loured upon our house' and now, ironically, they have returned.

Richard's order to 'bustle, bustle' is what he does best, keeping busy as he makes his plans. He is an experienced general, unlike Richmond, who 'was never trained up in arms'. Richard orders his horse to be covered in rich trappings and sets out his battle plan. He seems to recover his confidence as he prepares for battle. Traditional productions made Richard's recovery of confidence an important part of the play, but modern productions frequently show Richard as uncertain or desperate.

Richard dismisses the verse sent to Norfolk that accuses him of betrayal by accepting bribes as a trick by the enemy. He then attempts in a stirring oration to galvanise his troops into action. He portrays the enemy as an inferior and foreign army, destroying the land under a weak and inexperienced Richmond. When Richmond's forces are heard approaching, Richard utters his own rallying-cry to battle, urging the cavalry to fight so bravely that splinters from the wooden handles of their lances will fly into the sky:

> Fight, gentlemen of England! Fight boldly, yeomen!
> Draw, archers, draw your arrows to the head!
> Spur your proud horses hard and ride in blood;
> Amaze the welkin with your broken staves!   (lines 340–3)

News of Stanley's desertion to Richmond is a serious blow to Richard's battle plans. He ruthlessly orders George Stanley's head to be chopped off, but more urgent matters prevent the execution. Richard makes another impassioned appeal to his troops as Richmond's forces attack:

> Advance our standards! Set upon our foes!
> Our ancient word of courage, fair Saint George,
> Inspire us with the spleen of fiery dragons!
> Upon them! Victory sits on our helms!   (lines 350–3)

Act 5 Scene 4

Catesby attempts to rescue Richard, who has fought bravely, performing 'more wonders than a man'. Richard's horse is dead and he fights on foot, seeking Richmond 'in the throat of death' to slay him. He has gambled his crown on the successful outcome of the battle, but:

> I think there be six Richmonds in the field;
> Five have I slain today instead of him.
> A horse! a horse! my kingdom for a horse!   (lines 11–13)

In his moment of greatest need, the last king in Shakespeare's great history cycle is reduced to wanting only a horse.

Act 5 Scene 5

Richard's death gives the director unlimited opportunities to stage not only a thrilling climax, but also a personal interpretation of the play. In one production, a ghost entered when Richard was about to kill Richmond, saying 'Despair and die', and draining Richard of his power. In another Royal Shakespeare Company production, Margaret appeared, and her presence enabled Richmond to administer the deathblow. On film, McKellen played Richard standing in a jeep, and like a World War II general, commanding tanks and automatic weapons.

Richmond's comment on Richard ('the bloody dog is dead') echoes Margaret's words 'That I may live and say the dog is dead' (Act 4 Scene 4, line 78): the cycle of murder and revenge has at last ended with Richard's death. Richmond's crowning ('Wear it, and make much of it') marks the end of the Wars of the Roses and the beginning of the Tudor dynasty.

Richmond's final actions and language are intended to bring peace after a bloody civil war. He enquires after George Stanley, orders the proper burial of the nobles, and offers pardon to enemy soldiers who submit to him. His marriage to Elizabeth will unite the houses of York and Lancaster. He prays that the marriage will bring heirs and peace and prosperity to the country, and that traitors will never cause civil war again.

Critics differ over the quality and sincerity of Richmond's closing lines. One called them 'pious twaddle', while another claimed Richmond 'refers to all things an Elizabethan cared about'. On stage, director Michael Bogdanov (1987) plunged the stage into momentary darkness as Richard shouted his final, agonised cry for a horse. Immediately after, Richmond, dressed in gold, overcame Richard in a stylised, heroic contest. But Bogdanov subverted Richmond's courageous victory by setting his final speech as a political broadcast in a television studio. Bogdanov's interpretation suggests that Richmond may be more sophisticated than Richard, but he represents a continuation of political tyranny.

Act 5: Critical review

The oppositions that dominate the play are resolved in the final act. The long Scene 3 with its alternating episodes provides a strong dramatic contrast between the two sides. The wider conflict between Richard and God, Richard and Richmond, of good against evil and tyrant against saviour, is reflected in other contrasts: willing soldiers against fearful followers; sun against shadow; restlessness against calm; sweet sleep against nightmares. The ghosts wish Richard to 'Despair and die' and Richmond to 'Live and flourish'. Richard attempts to control Stanley through fear and coercion; Richmond wins his loyalty through genuine affection and family ties.

The language reflects that opposition. Richard's words portray a mind under pressure. He admits fear and uncertainty for the first time, is frequently confused, and when he awakes from his nightmares his diction and syntax powerfully reveal a mind disintegrating. Richmond's language brims over with confidence, for he is God's agent, ridding the land of a tyrant to bring peace to a ravaged country, to fulfil his role in the Tudor myth.

Powerful images reinforce the differences between the opposing sides. Richmond characterises Richard as a 'usurping boar' who is ravaging England. Richmond is associated with peace, trust and hope. Richard is associated with shadow, Richmond with fair weather. Richard's image of the 'blind cave of eternal night' contrasts with the 'sweet' and 'good' of Richmond. Richard's agonised outpourings as he awakens from his nightmare contrast with Richmond's 'sweetest sleep'.

Sleep and dreams can reveal the future. Clarence was reminded of his past crimes through a dream; Hastings foolishly ignored a dream; Buckingham accepts Richard's victims will mock him on a holy day. Richard is now forced to examine his conscience through his dream as those eleven victims that will mock Buckingham appear as ghosts to remind him (and the audience) of his terrible crimes. In a telling contrast to Buckingham, who retains his Christian belief, Richard defies his conscience and reaffirms his isolation from both the human and the divine. Choosing to be a villain, he will remain true to himself and die a villain, brave and defiant to the last.

Contexts

King Richard III was extremely popular in Shakespeare's time. Originally printed in 1597, it was reprinted in different versions (see page 74) no fewer than eight times in the following 30 years. There are also many references to the play in surviving documents of the period. What did Shakespeare's contemporaries find in the play that so interested them? Why did they find the play so fascinating?

The reason for the play's popularity among the Elizabethans seems to be that it was not simply good entertainment, but it reflected the social and political unease of the time and engaged with many of the anxieties of its first audiences. The play directly addresses the sense of English nationhood that was so encouraged by the Tudors, but was now made uneasy by growing anxieties about who would succeed the ageing Queen Elizabeth I. It questions the power of kingship and good and evil (morality). The play reflects the constant interest in religion, and its relationship to the state.

Shakespeare's imagination was fired by many of these important contemporary issues and he synthesised his experiences of them into his plays. This chapter examines particular factors that influenced him and his writing, and their contexts. Although these overlap they are treated separately as:

- Power politics and the Tudor myth
- Religion
- Theatre
- Everyday life in Shakespeare's England

This section concludes by asking 'What did Shakespeare write?'

Power politics and the Tudor myth

Shakespeare lived most of his life under the Tudors, whose concern was to establish the right of their dynasty to rule. To achieve that legitimacy, Richard must be portrayed as a bad king, who deserved to be overthrown by the first Tudor – Henry VII.

The new King Henry VII's claims to the throne were insecure. At a time of primogeniture (where first-born males succeed and inherit by right), he traced his royal ancestry back to John of Gaunt, Duke of Lancaster, through a female link. His male ancestor was Owen Tudor, an obscure Welsh squire who had married the widow of King Henry V. With such a questionable claim to the English throne it became essential for Henry to destroy Richard's reputation.

Under Henry VII and his son Henry VIII, successive historians and writers established the now traditional view of Richard as an evil, unpopular king. Chroniclers related events from the Tudor point of view. This perspective emphasised the horrors of the civil war, declared the legitimacy of the Tudor dynasty and praised the Tudors as the bringers of peace and prosperity to England.

During the reign of Henry VII, writers stressed that Richard was a usurper, who had no claim to the crown and who had murdered Henry VI, the princes in the Tower and his wife Anne. Even in 1483, two years before the Battle of Bosworth, an account was written by Dominic Mancini, an Italian priest, calling Richard a usurper.

History writing of the time was not the rigorous discipline that it is today. Historians felt that it was quite permissible to have a selective view of historical events to teach political and moral lessons. Two such 'histories' written during the reign of Henry VIII were responsible for the popular image of Richard as the evil hunchback:

- Sir Thomas More's unfinished book *History of Richard III* (1513–15) presents Richard as deformed, evil from birth and plotting to become king. More was born in 1478 and would have known many of Richard's contemporaries. In his youth, More served in the household of Morton, Bishop of Ely, who was a leading opponent of Richard (see Act 4 Scene 3, lines 49–50). More probably inherited Morton's prejudices. He provides Shakespeare with the vivid details of Richard gnawing his lip and having been born with teeth, and also provides some of the most dramatic scenes in the play (the arrest of Hastings in Act 3 Scene 4 and the scene with Buckingham in Act 3 Scene 5).
- Polydore Vergil's *Anglica Historia* (1534) was written at the request of Henry VIII to legitimise the Tudor dynasty. Vergil's argument expresses what has come to be called the Tudor myth. It claims that Henry IV's seizing of the crown from Richard II broke the God-given order of the universe and resulted in all the disasters that followed: the early death of Henry V, the bloody civil Wars of the

Roses and Richard III's murderous, despotic reign. Vergil claimed that England was rescued by Henry Tudor as God's instrument on earth, bringing peace and plenty by uniting the houses of York and Lancaster.

Under Queen Elizabeth, the historians Edward Hall and Raphael Holinshed incorporated the interpretations of More and Vergil into their history books. Hall's *Union of the Two Noble and Illustre Famelies of Lancastre and York* (1548) incorporated More's account. Holinshed then adapted Hall's account into his two editions of *Chronicles of England* (1577 and 1587). Hall and Holinshed incorporated the interpretations of More and Vergil so completely into their history books that by the end of the sixteenth century their very negative portrayal of Richard's appearance and actions was almost universally accepted. Their version of history was Shakespeare's major resource as he wrote his play.

Another source for *King Richard III* is *The Mirror for Magistrates*. This was an English anthology of biographies in verse, published in seven versions between 1559 and 1616. Most tales retold the cruel and ruinous lives of tyrants whose end was often violent. It was intended to teach moral lessons on how not to rule. The first two compilations dealt with material from Richard II onwards, and provided Shakespeare with details for his history plays. He may have used it for passages spoken by Richard, Clarence, Hastings, Edward IV and Buckingham.

History into drama

From his reading of the sources listed above, Shakespeare selected events and transformed them into an imaginative and gripping drama. The following represent some of his compressions, adaptations and reworkings as he wrote *King Richard III*:

- Clarence was an unstable character who not only suggested that his brother Edward was illegitimate, but also instigated riots against him. He was arrested and tried for treason in 1478 and condemned to death. His mother begged for him not to be publicly executed and three contemporary writers agree that he was put to death by being drowned in a butt of malmsey wine in the Tower of London. This was five years before the death of Edward IV.
- Henry VI's funeral (1471) actually occurred seven years before Clarence's death.

- Queen Margaret was exiled to France in 1476 and died in 1482 without returning to England. Shakespeare represents her as alive and in England until just before the Battle of Bosworth (1485).
- Anne was never married to Prince Edward. She was betrothed, which was a binding contract, but Edward died the year before she married Richard in 1472.
- Hastings would never have known about the fate of Grey, Rivers and Vaughan as he was executed nearly two weeks before them.
- Shakespeare compresses events into five scenes in Act 5. Buckingham was executed in November 1483, but it wasn't until August 1485 that Richmond successfully landed in England and the Battle of Bosworth took place on 22 August 1485.
- Did Richard kill the princes? Tudor legend portrayed Richard as a child-murderer, but the only historical evidence is that the Duke of York joined the young King Edward in the Tower on 16 June 1483. They were never seen again. Controversy still rages over what happened to the princes and many people protest that Richard was innocent of their deaths (notably in papers produced by the Society for the Friends of Richard III and in two novels by Josephine Tey – *The Daughter of Time* and *Dickon*).

Many critics attribute the play's enduring fascination to its compelling portrayal of *realpolitik*: what individual and social life is like under a despotic and brutal king ruling a deeply corrupt state. Exploiting the divisions caused by feuding political factions and the manipulation of individuals and the system, the calculating Richard seizes the opportunity to make himself king. He is a Machiavellian figure (see page 67), a cynical politician who uses any method to gain and maintain power.

The England of Elizabeth I contained similar ambitious nobles who jockeyed for power and position. The Earl of Essex, a long-time favourite of Queen Elizabeth I, attempted to raise a rebellion against the queen in 1601, but it failed miserably and Essex was executed. Today, *King Richard III* offers parallels with figures in our own time whose huge ambition has led to them to use ruthless means to achieve their goal. From this viewpoint Richmond could be seen, for all his talk of peace and unity, as yet another violent magnate, staging a coup to gain ultimate control of a profoundly unjust state.

Religion

Religion was all-pervasive in Elizabethan England, influencing every aspect of life and used by the state as an instrument to legitimise its role. *King Richard III* uses history to portray the Tudor myth and reveals the working of divine providence over nine decades, mirroring humankind's fall and redemption within this God-given scheme. This section shows some of the ways in which the play reflects religious concerns of the time.

Sin and salvation: 'The deed you undertake is damnable'

Since Henry VIII's break with Rome in the 1530s, with the exception of the six-year reign of Queen Mary, England had been a Protestant country. But many citizens still adhered to Catholicism and some critics suggest Shakespeare was a Catholic, based on evidence in his plays. *King Richard III* incorporates the Catholic notions of purgatory and confession. These arose from the belief that the soul lives after death and may be rewarded or punished by God. All hope of everlasting salvation depends on the individual's spiritual state at the moment of death. If all sins are confessed and forgiven by a priest (shriven) or the sacrament of bread and wine celebrated, the person dies in a state of grace and the soul enjoys an eternity of peace in heaven. To die with grave sins unconfessed and unforgiven damns the soul to everlasting suffering in hell. Those who had not fully confessed before dying were placed in purgatory (limbo) where they suffered remorse until the unconfessed minor sins were burnt away (purged).

Characters in the play are constantly reminded of their past sins. Richard recalls Margaret's cruel acts against his family (Act 1 Scene 3). Margaret's curses and prophecies remind the feuding nobles of their past crimes (Act 1 Scene 3). 'Your friends at Pomfret, they do need the priest' (Act 3 Scene 2, line 114) and 'Make a short shrift; he longs to see your head' (Act 3 Scene 4, line 94) emphasise the importance of eternal salvation. Clarence, Rivers, Hastings and Buckingham all refer to the importance of prayer, confession of sins and divine forgiveness before they die.

Conscience: 'Where's thy conscience now?'

With the growth of Protestantism under the Tudors, the notion of the importance of individual conscience became supremely important to the Elizabethans. Conscience gives the characters in the play an innate sense of what is right and wrong, especially in relation to their actions and motives. It strips away outward show to reveal their true feelings. The word 'guilt' (a symptom of conscience) occurs more often in *King Richard III* than any other Shakespeare play. Richard takes a deliberate decision to ignore the constraints of morality: 'I am determinèd to prove a villain' (Act 1 Scene 1, line 30). The night before Bosworth, tormented by his conscience, he awakes in terror from a nightmare. Clarence is troubled by conscience as he remembers his past crimes; the Second Murderer reflects on the power of conscience and repents Clarence's murder (Act 1 Scene 4). King Edward's last words reveal Clarence's murder weighing on his conscience. Tyrrel's account of the murder of the princes shows the remorse of Forrest and Dighton: 'Hence both are gone; with conscience and remorse' (Act 4 Scene 3, line 20).

Church versus state: 'The great King of kings'

Queen Elizabeth I's father, King Henry VIII, had declared himself the supreme head of the Church in an effort to bring the Church under royal control. But tension between Church and state was a constant source of friction, and the play exposes that tension. The belief in the 'divine right of kings' held that the monarch was God's representative on earth; a crime against the king was a crime against God. The crown, orb, sceptre and anointing with holy oil at a monarch's coronation symbolised the bond between the spiritual (Church) and the secular (state).

The play constantly reminds the audience of the powerlessness of Church against state when the king, who is God's representative on earth, is evil. Richard's hellish origins ('cacodemon', 'hell-hound') contrast with references to heaven, angels and saints that resonate throughout the play. Witnessing a succession of churchmen lending their holy office for Richard's advancement creates episodes rich in irony. The Bishop of Ely anxiously goes to gather strawberries for his monarch (Act 3 Scene 4); 'two bishops' support the 'pious' Richard (Act 3 Scene 7); and 'the grossness of this age' (Act 3 Scene 1, line 46) forces the Duke of York out of the sanctuary of the church to his death. Sanctuary was an age-old right of the persecuted to claim shelter and safety in a church. In Richard's England, the Church is rendered impotent.

Richard as Antichrist: 'And seem a saint, when most I play the devil'

Characters who are not fooled by Richard's outward appearance often react to him with different levels of fear and horror. Such evil is characteristic of the devil. Richard has disassociated himself from everyone. He is ruthlessly anti-Christian, deliberately setting himself against God and inverting the Christian values of love and forgiveness. He is cruel, pitiless, vicious, unforgiving and ultimately blasphemous in his mock piety. Elizabethan audiences would recognise him as the devil, the opposite of all Christian values, and many critics argue he represents the Antichrist.

Richard as the 'Scourge of God', 'hell's black intelligencer'

Despite his nature Richard becomes king and is the representative of God on earth. Theology was forced to reconcile the belief in a good and just God with a country suffering under a cruel and tyrannical king. Their response shaped the concept of the 'Scourge of God', a ruler who freely chose to punish a sinful people. Once the country was chastised, the king was in turn destroyed. A just king then replaced him, citizens were ever mindful of their past sins and lived in peace under the new king with divine justice restored. Richmond (the just king) rescues a scourged nation from Richard (the Antichrist and 'Scourge of God'). Richmond hints at this when he proclaims Richard has 'ever been God's enemy' (Act 5 Scene 3, line 253) and declares Richard's fall is divinely sanctioned (Act 5 Scene 5).

Theatre

Shakespeare experienced and absorbed an enormous variety of theatre that ranged from early Church morality plays to the bloodthirsty revenge dramas of the early 1590s. Those influences are reflected in this intensely dramatic play. This section examines some of the influences on Shakespeare as he was writing *King Richard III* and looks at how some critics believe the play is about the very nature of drama.

Seneca (4 BC–AD 65)

A collection of plays by the Roman dramatist Seneca was published in 1581, and enjoyed huge popular success on stage. Seneca found the material for his tragic dramas in Greek mythology, but his reworking of those ancient tales was done in a startling manner that greatly appealed to Elizabethan audiences. Seneca's plays contain:

- a chorus that comments on the action;
- ghosts and the supernatural;
- prophecies, omens and a vivid description of the underworld;
- a curse that predates the action;
- violence, bloodshed and physical horrors;
- the Furies (avenging goddesses who came from hell to punish and torment those guilty of terrible crimes). Queen Margaret resembles a Fury as she urges the characters to bloodshed and revenge. She is also the voice of nemesis (retribution), a defining feature of classical drama where the inevitable workings of fate brought death and suffering;
- soliloquies providing moments of reflection and self-examination.

The Church and the popular English drama

In earlier times the Church had been an important source of theatre. When there were few books and most of the population was illiterate, biblical and moral stories were dramatised to show the conflict between good and evil. These morality plays have stock figures:

The Devil

The arch-villain and the representative of evil who tempts people to sin so they will be punished for ever in hell. Richard's hellish origins ('cacodemon', 'hell-hound') stress his devilish nature and contrast with saintly Richmond, who ends Richard's evil reign. Some critics interpret the play as a contest of good against evil.

The Vice

The many sins that burden mankind were individually personified in earlier morality plays, but by the middle of the sixteenth century they were combined into a single representative figure of evil, named 'The Vice'. He is one of the devil's representatives and he takes a theatrical delight in trapping people into sin by charm, wit and double-dealing. Evidence suggests that his greatest popularity was between 1550 and 1580, when he became the star turn of morality plays. This character always had at least two names: one that represents his real, vicious nature (he is called 'Iniquity' in two plays performed in the 1560s, a name Richard applies to himself in Act 3 Scene 1, lines 82–3) and another that represents his duplicitous, seemingly innocuous or favourable nature ('Richard'). Much of the humour in *King Richard III* is based on the Vice's characteristic style. Like Richard, the Vice often takes pleasure in sharing his plotting with an audience. His bustling energy, delight in double meanings and wordplay, grotesque appearance, rapid plotting to escape detection and eventual punishment have much in common with Richard.

King Herod

Herod was another favourite character from medieval plays. His story is recounted in the Bible. Herod felt his position as ruler threatened when told of the birth of Jesus and of his title 'King of kings'. To protect his kingship, he ordered the deaths of all the male babies born in his kingdom of Judea (the infamous act of butchery that forever afterwards is referred to as 'the massacre of the Innocents'). In morality plays this evil tyrant was transformed into a comical character, whose ranting, shouting and over-played violence was another audience favourite. The murder of the princes in the Tower would remind an Elizabethan audience of Herod's evil act.

The Three Marys

Three female figures (Mary Magdalene, Mary Salome and Mary, the mother of James) are associated with the most significant and solemn moment of Christianity: Christ's rising from the dead three days after his crucifixion (the Resurrection). Medieval Resurrection plays re-enacted three episodes: the three women lament as they come to Christ's tomb, learn of the Resurrection from an angel, then give out the news of what they have learnt. Critics identify a similar pattern in three episodes of *King Richard III*: Elizabeth, the Duchess of York and Clarence's daughter lament Richard's victims (Act 2 Scene 2); Elizabeth, the Duchess and Anne approach the tomb: the Tower of London (Act 4 Scene 1); Elizabeth, the Duchess and Margaret proclaim Richard's evil deeds (Act 4 Scene 4). Some critics argue that Elizabethan audiences would associate the Three Marys with the women in the play. Some also point to the inversion of the original material, where celebration in the Resurrection plays is transformed into lamenting in *King Richard III*, with its purpose of emphasising Richard's terrible crimes and taking sympathy away from him.

Contemporary theatrical influences

Christopher Marlowe (1564–93)

Of all contemporary dramatists, Marlowe had the most important influence on Shakespeare. His plays often reflect his life: violent, dissolute and dramatic. Generally supposed by many to be an atheist, Marlowe believed religion was a mere plot 'to keep men in awe'. Critics agree that Richard has much in common with Marlowe's anti-heroes, especially the diabolic sadism of Barabas (*The Jew of Malta*, 1589) and the anti-Christian Tamburlaine (*Tamburlaine*, 1587). *Tamburlaine* also successfully established blank verse (see page 87) as the standard verse pattern for drama.

Popular opinion claimed that the Italian writer Niccolò Machiavelli (1469–1527) was much admired by Marlowe. Machiavelli argues in his book *The Prince* (1513) that politics must be separated from ethics, and for a ruler morality is unimportant, as the end justifies the means. Conscience is unimportant compared to the necessities of state and policy. The popular belief was that Machiavelli urged rulers to lie, deceive and even murder to retain their power – but put on a false face of religious piety and virtue.

Marlowe created two characters based on these principles: Barabas in *The Jew of Malta* and Faustus in *Doctor Faustus*. Their love of power and mischief-making, quick wit, magnetic personalities and habit of gloating self-congratulation anticipate many of the characteristic features of Richard. Richard states that he can 'set the murderous Machiavel to school' (*Henry VI Part 3*, Act 3 Scene 2, line 193) and *King Richard III* demonstrates how he fulfils that boast.

Thomas Kyd (1558–94)

Of all the plays inspired by Seneca, by far the most successful in the early 1590s was Thomas Kyd's *The Spanish Tragedy*. It was both extremely bloodthirsty and a searching examination of the relationship between revenge and justice, focusing on the working out of revenge. 'Revenge tragedies' such as this influenced *King Richard III*, as characters strive for justice and retribution.

The True Tragedie of Richard the Third

This play about Richard III, by an anonymous author, was published in 1594 but probably written earlier. Many critics believe that Shakespeare borrowed some ideas from it. The most obvious anticipates Richard's famous lines at Bosworth (Act 5 Scene 4, lines 7–10):

KING   A horse, a horse, a fresh horse.
PAGE   A flie my Lord, and saue your life
KING   Flie villaine, look I as tho I would flie

King Henry VI Part 3 (see also pages 4, 10, 74 and 90)

Shakespeare's earlier plays provided him with source material for *King Richard III*. In *Henry VI Part 3* Richard first emerges as the arch-villain. At first he fights bravely in the Wars of the Roses, but by the end of the play he is using soliloquies to proclaim his deformity, his lack of love (Act 3 Scene 2, lines 153–8), and his ambition to seize the crown (Act 3 Scene 2, lines 174–9).

Richard III is a play about acting

The play reflects the often corrupt times of late Elizabethan England. Personal ambition and lust for power generate hypocrisy, dishonesty and a lack of trust. Courtiers have to hide their true allegiances and feelings in order to survive. Shakespeare and his fellow dramatists reflected these difficult times in their plays, where words frequently hide the truth and a person can only be truly known through his actions.

References to plays and acting abound in dramatic language: 'inductions', 'Vice', 'deep tragedian', 'part', 'dissemble', 'tragedy', 'pageant'. The play's preoccupation with appearance and reality, pretence and seeming, echoes the nature of drama itself. Some critics describe *King Richard III* as metatheatre (theatre about theatre) or metadrama (drama about drama). They point out that many characters in the play are aware they are playing a role and stress the play's knowing self-awareness that it is an artificial creation. Some of the ways in which the text helps productions to remind the audience of the metadrama are now discussed.

Richard knowingly plays the actor, someone who pretends. He is the arch-deceiver and his skills as actor and manipulator enable him to use false words and appearances to fool other characters. His enthusiasm for sharing these skills with an audience, while other characters are on stage and unaware of what is happening, provides much of the play's fascination. Not all the characters are taken in by his deceptions. His mother has no doubt about his ability to 'dissemble' (Act 2 Scene 2, lines 31–2) for he has pretended, acted and lied to Clarence's children. Margaret sees Richard for what he is. Her first aside directed at Richard calls him a 'devil' (Act 1 Scene 3, line 116) and throughout the play she warns all who will listen of his evil nature.

But Richard remains the consummate actor as he plots to seize the crown. He plays many roles: devoted brother to Clarence (Act 1 Scene 1); devoted wooer of Anne (Act 1 Scene 2); the plain man who cannot flatter and the innocent unjustly accused (Act 1 Scene 3, lines 42–53 and 55–61); the grieving brother, shocked at the news of Clarence's death (Act 2 Scene 1, lines 78–81); one who shows mock amiability followed by mock fury with Hastings at the council meeting (Act 3 Scene 4).

Richard is even more audacious in his role-play as Buckingham joins him (Act 3). They wear old and rusty armour ('rotten armour, marvellous ill-favoured') in a melodramatic pretence to fool the Lord Mayor that they are under attack from supporters of the executed Hastings (Act 3 Scene 5). Their preparations are thorough. They artfully simulate danger by parodying contemporary Elizabethan tragedy, listing at least twelve of the techniques used by the great tragic actors including: 'quake', 'change colour', 'ghastly looks'. They add stage business as they see and hear imaginary attackers. Richard shouts 'Look back, defend thee, here are enemies!' (Act 3 Scene 5, line 19) and Hastings' severed head is brought on stage at the appropriate dramatic moment. The on-stage audience (the Lord Mayor) is persuaded to believe the pair of rogues and the theatre audience is delighted by such a dazzling display.

The metadrama continues in Act 3 Scene 7. Richard is directed to act as if he is afraid ('intend some fear') and 'get a prayer book in your hand' as Catesby and Buckingham unite in tricking the Lord Mayor and citizens. The simulation of fearful piety as Richard appears between two bishops brings Richard the prize of the crown of England.

Richard is not the only character who hides true feelings beneath an outward false show. Stanley successfully hides his true motives from Richard. Queen Elizabeth does not reveal her true intentions for her daughter's marriage. Appearance and reality are blurred as churchmen unwittingly ally themselves to an evil king. But one churchman does knowingly conceal his true allegiance: the Bishop of Ely fetches Richard strawberries, but later joins Richmond. Perhaps most poignantly (Act 3 Scene 1) neither Edward nor the Duke of York appear to believe Richard as they make their way to the Tower.

Queen Margaret's role is also integral to the metadrama. Echoing her roots in Greek drama (see pages 16, 65 and 72) she not only acts in and witnesses Richard's tyranny, but is a spectator at the prologue to a tragic performance:

> A dire induction am I witness to,
> And will to France, hoping the consequence
> Will prove as bitter, black, and tragical.
>
> (Act 4 Scene 4, lines 5–7)

Margaret describes Queen Elizabeth as acting a part over which she has no control. She is a 'painted queen' in a 'direful pageant' and 'A queen in jest, only to fill the scene' (Act 4 Scene 4, line 91). Hastings is a spectator at a tragedy when he complacently observes the fate of Rivers, Grey and Vaughan: 'I live to look upon their tragedy' (Act 3 Scene 2, line 59). A similar misfortune will later befall others, including Buckingham and Hastings himself, as the 'tragedy' or 'counterfeit' catches up with each.

Everyday life in Shakespeare's England

The play provides a fascinating glimpse into contemporary Elizabethan life. It reveals many of the preoccupations of Tudor England, such as concerns over status and the role of women in society.

Social hierarchy

The social system in Shakespeare's time was changing from the rigid four-class feudal system of gentlemen, citizens, yeomen and labourers/artificers into a more flexible status system. In the sixteenth century, fresh nobility was created to coexist with the old noble families. Monarchs, grateful for services rendered, ennobled successful merchants and lawyers. There was movement across class barriers. This evolving, more flexible class system is reflected in *King Richard III*. The old gentry often disliked the new nobles; Richard's comments about Queen Elizabeth and her parvenu family, with their relatively humble origins and recently attained wealth, would be typical of the thoughts of many of the old noble families:

> Since every jack became a gentleman,
> There's many a gentle person made a jack.
>
> *(Act 1 Scene 3, lines 71–2)*

Gentlemen were divided into several categories, from the monarch down to the person of lowest status, who was simply given the title 'gentleman'. It is this low status that Richard refers to when he talks of marrying Clarence's daughter to 'some mean poor gentleman' (Act 4 Scene 2, line 54). The 'jacks' becoming gentlemen refers to the higher-status characters, for example Richard's sneering remarks addressed to *Lord* Rivers and the *Marquess* of Dorset; Rivers and Dorset have relatively lowly origins, despite their fancy new titles. Throughout the play Richard sneers at those he considers below him in status (particularly women), for he is the 'eagle' who soars above the unimportant 'wrens'.

Social status of women

The play reveals the powerlessness of women and their dependence on men for influence. Queen Margaret was the once powerful wife of Henry VI. After his murder, she becomes a spectator and commentator on the action. Elizabeth exercised her considerable influence when she was queen to secure preferment for her family, but on Edward's death is forced to seek the security of sanctuary for both herself and her son. Anne becomes Richard's queen, but appears only once after the wooing scene to tell of her unhappiness and approaching death (Act 4 Scene 1).

Women may lose their social and political power when husbands die or tire of them, but they soon find other means of establishing their influence. Margaret is full of hatred and venom, but her mission succeeds, for all her curses prove true. The women in the play learn the importance of mutual feminine support as Margaret passes on her power of cursing to the Duchess of York and Elizabeth (Act 4 Scene 4). This gives the Duchess the power to publicly curse her son and Elizabeth the strength to face Richard as he tries to win her daughter's hand. Feminist critics argue that it is the women in the play who publicly expose Richard's corruption and tyranny when he is king by using the only weapons available to them: words (see pages 45 and 97).

Imprisonment and freedom

The menacing Tower of London would be a familiar sight to Elizabethan Londoners and they would be all too familiar with its bloody history. The Tower dominates much of the play. In a telling dramatic moment (Act 1 Scene 1) Hastings is released from the Tower as Clarence becomes its prisoner. The Tower comes to represent the arbitrary nature of imprisonment, which is subject to the will of the king. Richard's enemies will be imprisoned and face execution as his reign becomes ever more brutal. The 'new-delivered Hastings' ironically observes to Richard that 'eagles' are imprisoned while 'kites and buzzards' are free. Richard comments that Clarence is 'franked up to fatting for his pains' (Act 1 Scene 3, line 314). York and Elizabeth are forced into seeking sanctuary (a loss of liberty) and both York and Prince Edward go to the Tower reluctantly, never to be seen again: 'I do not like the Tower, of any place' (Act 3 Scene 1, line 68). Hastings calls the Tower a 'slaughterhouse' (Act 3 Scene 4, line 85) and Elizabeth vainly entreats the Tower to show mercy (Act 4 Scene 1, lines 99–104).

Nemesis and fate

The play examines political and religious issues that would be familiar to Elizabethans, but it has also been interpreted as being about nemesis and the working of fate. Nemesis is retribution (the punishment for wrongdoing) and fate the power that makes that punishment inevitable. This was the defining pattern of Greek drama, where the workings of fate brought suffering and death.

In *King Richard III*, lamentation, cursing, dreams, prophecies and omens, often written in stylised and ritualistic form, express the hatred and desire for retribution that dominates many episodes. The 'prophetess' Queen Margaret is the 'voice' of nemesis as she remembers past bloody deeds that call out for revenge. She prophesies that vengeance shall fall on the house of York for the wrongs done to the house of Lancaster (Act 1 Scene 3). As Richard's victims face death, each remembers Margaret's prophecy. When she again appears (Act 4 Scene 4) the audience is forced to recollect the force of her predictions.

Her final curse is for Richard as he nears his 'piteous and unpitied end' (Act 4 Scene 4, line 74).

But if Margaret is the voice of nemesis, Richard is its agent. He has the political power to destroy his enemies. Richard is at the centre of the action as death follows death, but he fails to see that he is part of the pattern and it is inevitable that he too must die. Richard describes his own fate to Elizabeth, ironically unaware of its truth (Act 4 Scene 4, lines 402–10).

Dreams and omens

Dreams and omens also belong to a world dominated by fate. Elizabethans believed that dreams revealed the future. Hastings wishes he had acted on Stanley's dream of the boar. The Elizabethan audience would understand Clarence's fear for his soul as he revealed his dream, and would know that Richard's nightmare guaranteed his defeat.

Omens are signs of coming events, often regarded as a threat or warning. Hastings ignores all omens. The Third Citizen warns of future strife ('Woe to that land that's governed by a child'). The young Duke of York's request for Richard's dagger is ominous, as is Richard's reply (Act 3 Scene 1, lines 111–12). The superficial attractiveness of strawberries (Act 3 Scene 4) and their emblematic association with snakes and the devil (see page 33) would alert an Elizabethan audience to Hastings' danger. Most potent of all are the omens the Duchess of York remembers and which she associates with Richard's birth: 'Thou cam'st on earth to make the earth my hell' (Act 4 Scene 4, line 167).

Witchcraft

During Queen Elizabeth's reign many people (nearly all women) were convicted as witches and suffered cruel punishment. Throughout Shakespeare's lifetime witches and witchcraft fascinated people and nearly everyone believed in witches. Richard's charge of witchcraft against Jane Shore would not have seemed unusual. Jane Shore was arrested for witchcraft after Richard's accusation and was put on trial. No evidence was found against her, but she was re-tried for harlotry and found guilty.

What did Shakespeare write?

Shakespeare wrote ten plays dramatising English history. Nine were written in the first ten years of his career, between 1589 and 1599. A further play was written with John Fletcher in about 1613 (*Henry VIII*). Of the first nine plays, one (*King John*) stands alone, whilst the remaining eight plays dramatise one continuous period of English history from 1398 to 1485. These plays are often referred to as Shakespeare's history cycle. Critics agree on the order in which the plays were written, but there is continuing debate on the exact dates of some plays in the cycle. The four plays portraying earlier events were actually written after the four plays dramatising later history.

King Richard III is the final play in the cycle portraying the struggle for the English crown. It dramatises the English civil war (called the Wars of the Roses) and continues the story begun in the three plays of *King Henry VI*. The following brief summaries of the earlier plays and the order in which they should be performed historically will help an understanding of how *King Richard III* relates to them:

- *King Richard II* (written in 1595) tells how Henry Bullingbrook deposes King Richard and is crowned as King Henry IV.
- *King Henry IV Parts 1 and 2* (written in 1596–97/8) tell of Prince Hal's exploits with Falstaff, his victory at Shrewsbury over Hotspur (Part 1) and how he finally rejects Falstaff when he becomes king (Part 2).
- *King Henry V* (written in 1599) tells of Henry's victory at Agincourt and his betrothal to Katherine, the French king's daughter.
- *King Henry VI Parts 1, 2 and 3* (written around 1589–91/2) tell how Henry loses the English possessions in France and sees his country racked by civil war (the Wars of the Roses) as a rival family, the house of York, challenges his right to rule. The Yorkists are triumphant.

King Richard III was probably first performed in London in either 1593 or 1594. What was the play that Shakespeare wrote and his audiences heard? No one knows for certain because his original text has not survived. A number of Shakespeare's plays were published in his lifetime: these are called Quarto volumes. A quarto page is about the same size as this page you are reading. The first edition of the play, known as the First Quarto, was printed in 1597. It was probably written out from memory by the actors when on a provincial tour and used as a prompt copy. The play was so popular that another seven Quarto editions were published over the 30 years which followed.

Shakespeare died in 1616. Seven years later, two former professional associates published his collected plays in one large volume. This edition is called the First Folio and remains the only authoritative source for about half the plays. A folio page is about two times larger than the page you are reading. The editors of the First Folio used the texts of the Third and Sixth Quarto printed editions, but scholars now believe they also had access to a (now lost) manuscript version of the play made for theatrical use, perhaps even a copy of Shakespeare's original.

The Folio and Quarto editions have many differences. A major discrepancy is that the Folio has more than 200 lines that are not present in the Quarto. Editors of the play debate which version is the most authentic. This explains why there are differences in the text of various modern editions of the play. There is no such thing as a definitive text, but rather there are several texts. Whichever text you are using will vary from what Shakespeare actually wrote. Every performance selects, cuts and emends to present its own unique version of *King Richard III*. This Guide follows the New Cambridge edition of the play (also used in Cambridge School Shakespeare), which is based on the First Folio and includes, in brackets, lines from the other six Quartos.

Language

Expressions from *King Richard III* have become universally known. Many phrases have passed into everyday speech: 'A horse, a horse, my kingdom for a horse!', 'Now is the winter of our discontent', 'Chop off his head', 'I'll have her, but I will not keep her long'.

But the language of the play is much more than a treasure house of quotations. It contains a wide variety of language registers. Simply listing a few types of language used can show its stylistic diversity: curses, lamentations, puns, oaths, repetitions, witty and sophisticated wordplay, proverbs, insults. *King Richard III* is an early play and the influence of Shakespeare's time at school, where rhetoric (the art of using language persuasively) was central to the curriculum, can be clearly seen.

Shakespeare's knowledge of rhetoric permeates the play as characters consciously use carefully structured arguments to try to achieve their aims. Buckingham successfully convinces the Woodvilles that a small escort should bring Prince Edward to London (Act 2 Scene 2, lines 125–32); the wooing scenes between Richard and Anne then Richard and Elizabeth employ persuasive arguments that rely on rhetoric.

As a schoolboy, Shakespeare imitated classical models, practising all kinds of ways of using language that he later employed in *King Richard III*. One such technique is called *stichomythia*. This is an imitation of the cut-and-thrust dialogue found in the plays of the first-century Roman playwright Seneca, in which rapidly alternating lines create a verbal duel. It has also been described as the 'rapid interchange of witty repartee' that emphasises the artificial quality of the argument. Shakespeare demonstrates his knowledge of this technique of classical drama in the wooing of both Anne (Act 1 Scene 2, lines 197–205) and Elizabeth (Act 4 Scene 4, lines 347–71).

Ben Jonson famously remarked that Shakespeare 'wanted art' (lacked technical skill). But his comment is mistaken, as is the popular image of Shakespeare as a 'natural' writer, utterly spontaneous, inspired only by his own imagination. Shakespeare possessed a profound knowledge of the language techniques of his own and previous times. Behind the apparent effortlessness of the language lies a deeply practised skill. What follows are some of the language techniques Shakespeare uses in *King Richard III* to intensify dramatic effect, create mood and character, and so produce memorable theatre. As you read them, always keep in mind that Shakespeare wrote for the stage, and that actors will therefore employ a wide variety of both verbal and non-verbal methods to exploit the dramatic possibilities of the language. They will use the full range of their voices and accompany the words with appropriate expressions, gestures and actions.

Imagery

King Richard III abounds in imagery: vivid words and phrases that help create the atmosphere of the play as they conjure up emotionally-charged mental pictures. Shakespeare seems to have thought in images, and the whole play richly demonstrates his unflagging and varied use of verbal illustration. Perhaps the most famous example is in the opening lines of the play, where Richard compares the 'winter' of the past war to the 'summer' of the present time of peace.

The play is rich in animal imagery. Richard is called 'dog', 'hedgehog', 'hell-hound', 'bunch-backed toad', 'bottled spider', 'cur', 'rooting hog', 'cockatrice' and compared insultingly to many animals throughout the play. Those who are imprisoned, like Clarence and Hastings, are 'mewed' like captive birds of prey, while those who are free and in power are 'kites and buzzards' or 'eagles'.

Early critics such as Doctor Johnson and John Dryden were critical of Shakespeare's fondness for imagery. They felt that many images obscured meaning and detracted attention from the subjects they represented. However, over the past 200 years critics, poets and audiences have increasingly valued Shakespeare's imagery (sometimes called 'figures' or 'figurative language'). They recognise how he uses it to give pleasure and stir the audience's imagination, deepening the dramatic impact of particular moments or moods, providing insight into character, and intensifying meaning and emotional force. Images carry powerful significance far deeper than their surface meanings. For example, Clarence describes the physical pain of drowning and the moment of death; the immeasurable wealth on the sea-bed and its worthlessness; the pain he feels as he wishes to die but is unable to do so:

CLARENCE   Oh Lord, methought what pain it was to drown,
          What dreadful noise of water in mine ears,
          What sights of ugly death within mine eyes.
          Methoughts I saw a thousand fearful wracks,
          A thousand men that fishes gnawed upon,
          Wedges of gold, great anchors, heaps of pearl,
          Inestimable stones, unvalued jewels,
          All scattered in the bottom of the sea.
          Some lay in dead men's skulls, and in the holes
          Where eyes did once inhabit there were crept,
          As 'twere in scorn of eyes, reflecting gems,
          That wooed the slimy bottom of the deep
          And mocked the dead bones that lay scattered by.
KEEPER   Had you such leisure in the time of death
          To gaze upon these secrets of the deep?
CLARENCE   Methought I had, and often did I strive
          To yield the ghost; but still the envious flood
          Stopped in my soul and would not let it forth
          To find the empty, vast, and wandering air,
          But smothered it within my panting bulk,
          Who almost burst to belch it in the sea.

                                   (Act 1 Scene 4, lines 21–41)

The vivid visual images of a world beneath the sea combined with the agony that makes Clarence long for death creates a nightmarish picture as Clarence's tormented soul journeys to hell.

A profusion of similarly memorable word pictures pervades the play. Caroline Spurgeon (a pioneering critic on Shakespeare's imagery), was particularly struck by the number of tree and garden images. She concludes that 'The royal house is definitely thought of as a tree with the children and kinsfolk as branches, leaves, flowers or fruit, and this idea of a tree being planted, shaken by storms, grafted, rooted up and withered is constantly present'. Queen Elizabeth, lamenting the death of King Edward, asks:

          Why grow the branches when the root is gone?
          Why wither not the leaves that want their sap?

                                   (Act 2 Scene 2, lines 41–2)

Shakespeare's imagery uses metaphor, simile and personification. All are comparisons which in effect substitute one thing (the image) for another (the thing being described).

A metaphor is a comparison, suggesting that two dissimilar things are actually the same. When Margaret says:

> From forth the kennel of thy womb has crept
> A hell-hound that doth hunt us all to death:
> That dog, that had his teeth before his eyes
> To worry lambs and lap their gentle blood
>
> *(Act 4 Scene 4, lines 47–50)*

she is using an extended metaphor. The image of Richard as a dog from hell is expanded and elaborated as the Duchess of York's womb becomes a 'kennel' to house the dog Richard, while the princes in the Tower are 'lambs', harassed and finally killed by him.

When Richard says:

> Our aerie buildeth in the cedar's top,
> And dallies with the wind and scorns the sun.
>
> *(Act 1 Scene 3, lines 264–5)*

he is comparing the house of York's high status to an 'aerie', a nest of young eagles (birds of prey). It was believed to be a sign of the noble nature of eagles that they could gaze into the sun without harming their sight. Richard is therefore stressing his own family's powerful stance as it gazes unblinkingly over everyone from its elevated position. To put it another way, a metaphor uses one word or phrase to express another idea. Queen Margaret powerfully compares Queen Elizabeth's brief enjoyment of power to her own by insulting Elizabeth as a 'vain flourish', 'a poor shadow', 'a breath', 'a bubble'.

A simile also compares one thing to another using 'like' or 'as'. For example, Richard claims he is 'like the formal Vice, Iniquity' (Act 3 Scene 1, line 82). The Second Murderer, shamed by his part in Clarence's death, says 'How fain, like Pilate, would I wash my hands / Of this most grievous murder' (Act 1 Scene 4, lines 264–5). Hastings says that one who seeks earthly fame 'Lives like a drunken sailor on a mast, / Ready with every nod to tumble down / Into the fatal bowels of the deep' (Act 3 Scene 4, lines 98–100). When Buckingham fails to convince the citizens, he says 'they spake not a word, / But like dumb statues or breathing stones / Stared each on other and looked deadly pale' (Act 3 Scene 7, lines 24–6).

Personification turns all kinds of things into persons, giving them human feelings or attributes. The two murderers call conscience 'blushing, shamefaced'. Richard speaks of 'dull delay' and 'snail-paced beggary'. The Duchess of York tells of England's earth 'made drunk'. The Tower of London is personified as cradle, nurse and companion by Queen Elizabeth as she invokes the menacing prison to care for her sons:

> Pity, you ancient stones, those tender babes
> Whom envy hath immured within your walls,
> Rough cradle for such little pretty ones.
> Rude, ragged nurse, old sullen playfellow
> For tender princes, use my babies well.
>
> *(Act 4 Scene 1, lines 99–103)*

Antithesis

Antithesis is the opposition of words or phrases against each other, as in 'Your grace attended to their sugared words / But looked not on the poison of their hearts.' (Act 3 Scene 1, lines 13–14). This setting of word against word ('attended to' is set against 'looked not on', 'sugared' against 'poison' and 'words' against 'hearts') is one of Shakespeare's favourite language devices. He uses it extensively in all his plays. Why? Because antithesis powerfully expresses conflict through its use of opposites, and conflict is the essence of all drama.

In *King Richard III*, conflict occurs in many forms: the supporters of King Edward against those of Queen Margaret; Richard against all who stand in his way to the throne; freedom against imprisonment; men against women; life against death; the past against the present and the future; heaven against hell; appearance against reality.

Antithesis intensifies the sense of conflict, and embodies its different forms. For example, Richard's soliloquy that opens the play contains many examples of antithesis in the first sixteen lines alone:

winter/summer   smoothed/wrinkled
bruisèd arms / monuments   mounting/capers
stern alarums / merry meetings   rudely stamped / love's majesty
dreadful marches / delightful measures

In the two wooing scenes the use of *stichomythia* (see page 76) produces balanced and antithetical pairings of sentences:

RICHARD   Your reasons are too shallow and too quick.
ELIZABETH   Oh, no, my reasons are too deep and dead,
    Too deep and dead, poor infants, in their graves.

(Act 4 Scene 4, lines 365–7)

Similarly, in Act 1 Scene 2 Anne uses the language of hell and vengeance, which contrasts with Richard's words of heaven and forgiveness, and bristles with antithesis:

ANNE   Oh, wonderful, when devils tell the truth!
RICHARD   More wonderful, when angels are so angry.
    Vouchsafe, divine perfection of a woman,
    Of these supposèd crimes to give me leave
    By circumstance but to acquit myself.
ANNE   Vouchsafe, diffused infection of man,
    Of these known evils but to give me leave
    By circumstance to curse thy cursèd self.   *(lines 73–80)*

Repetition

King Richard III is a highly patterned play. Early scenes often find a parallel with later ones. The successful wooing of Anne (Act 1 Scene 2) parallels the unsuccessful wooing of young Elizabeth (Act 4 Scene 4); Clarence's dream (Act 1 Scene 4) finds its counterpart in Richard's nightmare visit from the ghosts (Act 5 Scene 3); the murder of young Rutland (described in Act 1 Scene 3) is balanced by the murder of the princes in the Tower.

The search for order and justice through closely patterned acts, scenes and episodes is echoed in the language: 'Plantagenet doth quit Plantagenet', 'brother to brother', 'Blood to blood, self against self', 'Wrong hath but wrong, and blame the due of blame'.

But many other different forms of language repetitions run through the play, contributing to its atmosphere, creation of character and dramatic impact. Apart from the functional words ('the', 'and', etc.) many lexical words are frequently repeated: 'blood', 'grace', 'God', 'hate', 'hell', 'murder', 'Tower', 'guilt', 'Lord'. Their repetition is a clear indication of the major preoccupations of the play.

Shakespeare's skill in using repetition to heighten theatrical effect and deepen emotional and imaginative significance is most evident in particular speeches. Repeated words, phrases, rhythms and sounds add intensity to the moment or episode:

> Was ever woman in this humour wooed?
> Was ever woman in this humour won?
>
> *(Act 1 Scene 2, lines 231–2)*

The structural repetition reveals Richard's cynical delight and joy in his own cleverness in winning Anne. Some episodes have a ritualistic quality because of the symmetrical repetition of particular phrases and rhythms. The women express their sorrow in stylised, formal language (Act 4 Scene 4). Between lines 39 and 46 there are seven uses of 'killed' or 'kill':

MARGARET   I had an Edward, till a Richard killed him;
            I had a husband, till a Richard killed him.
            Thou hadst an Edward, till a Richard killed him;
            Thou hadst a Richard, till a Richard killed him.
DUCHESS   I had a Richard too, and thou didst kill him;
            I had a Rutland too, thou holp'st to kill him.
MARGARET   Thou hadst a Clarence, too,
            And Richard killed him.

The ghosts repeat the phrase 'despair and die' (Act 5 Scene 3) eight times before Buckingham's final curse from the grave:

> Dream on, dream on, of bloody deeds and death.
> Fainting, despair; despairing, yield thy breath.   *(lines 174–5)*

The ghosts hope Richmond will 'Live and flourish'. The cumulative effect of despair against hope and curse against blessing highlights the ritual aspects of the drama and points to Richard's inevitable downfall.

Particular examples of repetition are alliteration (the repetition of consonants at the beginning of words) and assonance (repeated vowel sounds). Both are evident in the single line:

> And with a virtuous visor hide deep vice.
>
> *(Act 2 Scene 2, line 28)*

Repetition also sometimes occurs in rhyme, which is used to achieve different effects. For example, Richard's total lack of feeling for his brother Clarence is given a grim humour by his use of rhyme:

> This day should Clarence closely be mewed up
> About a prophecy which says that 'G'
> Of Edward's heirs the murderers shall be.
>
> *(Act 1 Scene 1, lines 38–40)*

The same sense of closure is evident in the many scenes ending with a rhyming couplet, as in the First Murderer's last lines in Act 1 Scene 4:

> And when I have my meed, I will away,
> For this will out, and then I must not stay.   *(lines 275–6)*

or Buckingham's in Act 5 Scene 1:

> Come, lead me, officers, to the block of shame;
> Wrong hath but wrong, and blame the due of blame.
>
> *(lines 28–9)*

Lists

One of Shakespeare's favourite language methods is to accumulate words or phrases rather like a list. He had learnt the technique as a schoolboy in Stratford-upon-Avon, and his skills in knowing how to use lists dramatically are evident in the many examples in *King Richard III*. He intensifies and varies description, atmosphere and argument as he 'piles up' item on item, incident on incident. Sometimes the list consists almost entirely of single words, as in:

> Deep, hollow, treacherous, and full of guile
>
> *(Act 2 Scene 1, line 38)*

Richard and Buckingham list at least twelve techniques that a tragic actor should be able to do as they prepare to fool the Lord Mayor and citizens (Act 3 Scene 5). They must 'quake' and 'change colour'. They should be 'distraught' and 'mad with terror' as well as being able to 'Tremble' and have 'ghastly looks'.

The Duchess of York's description of Richard's life is a painful catalogue of a mother's perception of her son:

A grievous burden was thy birth to me.
Tetchy and wayward was thy infancy;
Thy schooldays frightful, desperate, wild, and furious;
Thy prime of manhood, daring, bold, and venturous;
Thy age confirmed, proud, subtle, sly, and bloody
(*Act 4 Scene 4, lines 168–72*)

Richard often uses lists to describe himself in ways he knows are false, but frequently cause laughter in an audience:

Because I cannot flatter and look fair,
Smile in men's faces, smooth, deceive, and cog,
Duck with French nods and apish courtesy,
I must be held a rancorous enemy.   (*Act 1 Scene 3, lines 47–50*)

The many lists in the play provide valuable opportunities for actors to vary their delivery. In speaking, an actor usually seeks to give each 'item' a distinctiveness in emphasis and emotional tone and sometimes adds an accompanying action and expression. In addition, the accumulating effect of lists can add to the force of an argument, enrich atmosphere, amplify meaning and provide extra dimensions of character.

Puns

A pun is a clever or humorous play on the meanings of words that sound or look similar. Shakespeare uses puns as a favourite device in all his plays, and *King Richard III* is rich in them. Richard is a master of the pun as he turns meaning on its head to ridicule, embarrass, sneer at or attack his opponents. He puns on 'son'/'sun' in the second line of the play. The 'son of York' is King Edward, but the 'sun' was also the Yorkist emblem that would bring light and warmth to their cause. Richard puns on the word 'naught/nought' when speaking of Jane Shore to Brakenbury:

BRAKENBURY   With this, my lord, myself have nought to do.
RICHARD   Naught to do with Mistress Shore? I tell thee, fellow,

He that doth naught with her (excepting one)
Were best to do it secretly alone.

(*Act 1 Scene 1, lines 97–100*)

For an Elizabethan audience 'naught' could mean 'except for one person', 'to do nothing' and 'to have sex with'.

Richard reveals his hatred of the Woodvilles by punning on 'noble' (Act 1 Scene 3, line 81) meaning 'one of nobility', but also 'a coin worth less than half an English pound'. A few lines later he outmanoeuvres Rivers when he puns on 'marry' (meaning 'by the Virgin Mary' or 'indeed' or 'to wed').

Anne's reference to Richard as a 'hedgehog' is a general term for an unfeeling person, but also refers to Richard's emblem of the hog. Hastings uses the word 'grace' to mean both 'good fortune' and 'God's forgiveness'. In an episode full of wordplay, young York mocks Richard when he puns on 'bear' (Act 3 Scene 1, lines 128–32). While meaning 'to carry', it also refers to Richard's hump, as trained bears carried apes on their shoulders that made them look hunchbacked. Throughout the play 'blood' can refer to family, gore, rage or the Yorkists in general and Richard in particular.

Oaths

An oath is a formal promise made in the name of a god or holy person, but Richard frequently turns it into an irreverent and blasphemous expression. Richard's favourite oath is to swear by St Paul. J Dover Wilson suggests that Shakespeare adopted this as Richard's habitual oath, because it adds to the mock piety that is one of the more entertaining masks that Richard assumes. Richard pretends piety when he wishes 'I would to God my heart were flint, like Edward's' (Act 1 Scene 3, line 138). But his inability to swear an oath to Elizabeth (Act 4 Scene 4) reveals his moral emptiness, for he respects nothing. In the final act, Richard's oaths ('Jesus' and 'By the apostle Paul') contrast with Richmond's many heartfelt invocations to God ('Then in God's name march!').

Clarence was guilty of perjury ('forswore himself') when he swore an oath before God that he later broke (Act 1 Scene 3, line 134). Anne swears 'With all my heart' to wear Richard's ring (Act 1 Scene 2, line 223). Stanley hopes that 'Pray God, I say, I prove a needless coward' in an ironic interchange with Hastings (Act 3 Scene 2, line 87).

Brakenbury is 'bound by oath' to let no one see the princes (Act 4 Scene 1, lines 27–8).

Biblical references

Like all Elizabethan schoolboys, the young Shakespeare was taught the Bible from an early age, and its influence is apparent throughout *King Richard III*:

> And thus I clothe my naked villainy
> With odd old ends stol'n forth of holy writ,
> And seem a saint when most I play the devil.
>
> *(Act 1 Scene 3, lines 336–8)*

Richard refers to Clarence ironically because he will 'shortly send thy soul to heaven' (Act 1 Scene 1, lines 118–20). He mocks the words of the marriage service ('to have and to hold') as he says of Anne 'I'll have her, but I will not keep her long' (Act 1 Scene 2, line 233). In the same scene he parodies St Matthew's gospel ('Bless them that curse you') when he speaks of 'blessings for curses'. Richard's blasphemous mock piety is again revealed in his lines 'Else wherefore breathe I in a Christian land?' (Act 3 Scene 7, line 115) as he addresses the wishes of the citizens.

Richard is not the only character to use the Bible for his own purpose. Anne's 'Or any creeping venomed thing that lives' (Act 1 Scene 2, line 20) parodies the line from the first book of the Bible ('every creeping thing that creepeth upon the earth'). Queen Margaret refers to heaven 'And there awake God's gentle sleeping peace' (Act 1 Scene 3, line 288) to add strength to her call for vengeance. The Third Citizen's warning ('Woe to that land that's governed by a child') echoes a line from the biblical book Ecclesiastes.

Irony

King Richard III is a play much concerned with false appearance. Shakespeare frequently uses both verbal irony and dramatic irony to underpin the contrast between what characters say and what they do. Richard is the master of verbal irony. Everything he says to Clarence and Hastings in the first scene of the play is loaded with double meaning. When he tells Clarence 'I will deliver you or else lie for you' Clarence thinks his brother promises to free him from prison or else take his place there. But Richard has murder and telling lies in mind (he will 'deliver' Clarence from life, rather than prison).

Dramatic irony is where the audience knows more than one or more of the characters on stage. The young York calls Richard 'gentle uncle' and 'kind uncle', unaware that his uncle wishes him dead. There is huge dramatic irony in the sight of the wicked Richard appearing between two churchmen: the contrast of all he has said and done against his pretended saintliness. Hastings' reply to Catesby stresses his foolishness, for the audience knows that what he says will actually happen: 'I'll have this crown of mine cut from my shoulders / Before I'll see the crown so foul misplaced' (Act 3 Scene 2, lines 43–4).

Verse and prose

There is very little prose in *King Richard III*, partly because it is an 'early' play (from the period when Shakespeare wrote mainly in verse) and partly because most of the characters belong to a royal household. Traditionally, theatrical convention decreed that high-status characters spoke in verse. Verse was also thought more suitable for tragedy. The only characters to speak in prose are the two murderers, who use prose when they argue with each other, but speak to Clarence in verse.

The verse of *King Richard III* is mainly blank verse: unrhymed verse written in iambic pentameter. It is conventional to define iambic pentameter as a rhythm or metre in which each line has five stressed syllables (/) alternating with five unstressed syllables (×):

> × / × / × / × / × /
> A horse! a horse! my kingdom for a horse!

At school, Shakespeare had learned the technical definition of iambic pentameter. In Greek *penta* means 'five', and *iamb* means a 'foot' of two syllables, the first unstressed, the second stressed, as in the pronunciation of 'alas': aLAS. Shakespeare practised writing in that metre, and his early plays, such as *Titus Andronicus* or *King Richard III* are very regular in rhythm (often expressed as de-DUM de-DUM de-DUM de-DUM de-DUM), with many lines 'end-stopped' (each making sense on its own):

> God and your arms be praised, victorious friends!
> The day is ours; the bloody dog is dead.

Traditional criticism

From the late eighteenth century, through the nineteenth and well into the twentieth, criticism of *King Richard III* has centred mainly on the character of its chief protagonist. The nineteenth-century critic Herman Ulrici writes of Richard existing outside the world of the play: 'As in life, so in the play, he (Richard) stands alone'. He argues that the play lacks 'the principle of interaction' because there is no real opposition to Richard in the first four acts, 'only submission and impotence'. Richard is seen as a study in tyranny, representing selfishness in its worst form. Other nineteenth-century critics write in a similar vein. Georg Gervinus believes that 'Richard fills the centre entirely' but for him it 'has given to this history (play) the character rather of a pure tragedy'. Edward Dowden views Richard as being 'of the diabolical (something more dreadful than the criminal) class'. To George Bernard Shaw, Richard is 'the prince of Punches' (from the children's puppet show 'Punch and Judy').

Much traditional criticism discusses Shakespeare's Richard as if he were a real person, rather than as Shakespeare's imagined character in a play. The critic most associated with character criticism is A C Bradley. Some 100 years ago, he delivered a course of lectures at Oxford University that were published in 1904 as *Shakespearean Tragedy*. The book has never been out of print, and Bradley's approach has been hugely influential. It expresses the spirit of much nineteenth-century criticism, and it determined the form of the majority of criticism for a good deal of the twentieth century. Today, modern critics judge Bradley's view of tragedy, with its emphasis on character, as simplistic, and they are uncomfortable with making moral judgements on characters.

But Bradley's view of tragedy has special application to the play. He sees tragedy as a process where, paradoxically, after catastrophe, order and unity are restored. Although there is conflict and waste, evil is eventually overcome. A tragedy's end may not be happy, but it promises something better ahead. Bradley did not write specifically about *King Richard III*, but his view of tragedy carried with it an almost universal application for all Shakespeare's tragic plays. The idea of suffering which must be endured under evil Richard before peace is restored by Richmond was a critical approach that remained popular for at least the next 60 years.

Character criticism continued throughout much of the twentieth century. Seven years after *Shakespearean Tragedy* was published, the poet John Masefield says that 'The intellect of Richard III is like that of Napoleon'. John Palmer thinks Richard is 'the eternal bully', and Alfred Harbage finds Richard an 'amusing devil'. Emrys Jones views Richard and Buckingham 'as gangsters . . . upper-class thugs', while W H Auden thinks Richard is not evil for personal gain, but that his 'primary satisfaction is in the infliction of suffering on others, or the power over others against their will'. Derek Traversi memorably describes Richard's decline in the last two acts as 'whistling in the dark to keep up his courage'.

Such was Bradley's influence that even critics associated with opening new critical approaches to Shakespeare often worked within Bradley's assumptions, particularly regarding character. But there were significant challenges. L C Knights mocks Bradley's emphasis on character in his essay 'How Many Children Had Lady Macbeth?' In *Shakespeare: The Histories* (1962) he stresses the importance of the structure, language and poetry of *King Richard III*, particularly its 'formal pattern', and writes 'I do not intend to take up again the question of "character" in Shakespeare'. Yet on the following page he writes that 'in some sense we feel them (the characters) as if they were persons'.

Even in the nineteenth century, the character approach was questioned. As early as 1885, Richard G Moulton wrote that 'Amongst ordinary readers of Shakespeare, Character-Interest, which is largely independent of performance, has swallowed up all other interests'. He stresses the importance of Shakespeare as a dramatist and the paramount importance of plot, and details that 'would be present to the eye of the spectator'. Moulton's interest lay in what he called 'English Drama' and whether the play should be classified as a tragedy or a history. In his *Shakespeare as a Dramatic Artist* he defines *King Richard III* as 'a sort of Christianised Greek tragedy' which emphasises not character, but plot.

Moulton was the first critic to establish the important influence on *King Richard III* of plays from early Greek theatre, and wrote the first classic description of the workings of nemesis and fate and their relationship to the plot of *King Richard III*. The play was one that 'presents to us the world of history transformed into an intricate design of which the recurring pattern is nemesis'. He describes how the wheel of nemesis revolves slowly yet irrevocably until all the guilty, including Richard, are punished.

Sixty years after Moulton's book (which had little influence in his own time) Lily B Campbell revisited the problem of classifying *King Richard III* as tragedy or history. She concludes that the distinction between history and tragedy is not clear, but her studies had an impact that was to have an incalculable influence on later criticism. She realises that the play must be interpreted in the historical context of the time at which it was written. She writes that 'the poet must be reckoned a man among men, a man who can be understood only against the background of his own time. His ideas and his experience are conditioned by the time and place in which he lives'. She was also convinced that 'Shakespeare's plots were clear and sure because he had a definite, fundamental conception of universal law'. By 'universal law' she meant the Tudor view of history (see page 59).

E M W Tillyard was the influential critic who attempted to define the 'universal law' that provided such clarity to Shakespeare's plots. A contemporary of Campbell, Tillyard also attempted to put the history plays into their historical context. His influential book *The Elizabethan World Picture* (1943) portrayed England as unified and harmonious. Tillyard claims it was a place where social order was maintained because almost everyone believed in 'the great chain of being' in which everything had its proper place. Tragedy arises when this natural order is overthrown. It was this idea that formed the basis of his later, equally influential book, *Shakespeare's Histories* (1944) and reaffirmed the idea of the Tudor myth.

Tillyard argues that *King Richard III* suffers when it is performed merely as a study of character, and can only be fully understood when considered alongside *King Henry VI Parts 1, 2 and 3* as the final play that concludes the events portrayed earlier. This is not only to clarify the plot, but also because:

> The greatest bond uniting all of the plays is the steady political theme: the theme of order and chaos, of proper political degree and civil war, of crime and punishment, of God's mercy finally tempering his justice, of the belief that such had been God's way with England.

Tillyard views Richmond as God's instrument to restore peace. Richmond's final speech 'would have raised the Elizabethans to an ecstasy of feeling' that would cause them to take 'the dramatist's final amen with a transport of affirmation'. Shakespeare's great sweep of history that ends with *King Richard III* reaffirms the idea of the Tudor myth, as the divine plan is finally revealed and 'saintly' Richmond restores a scourged England to political stability.

In Tillyard's interpretation, Shakespeare is writing a moral, patriotic and religious play that reflects the beliefs of all who watched it. He holds that *King Richard III* is a 'very religious play' because its structure relies heavily on the influence of the early English morality plays, and because it portrays the penitence of Clarence, King Edward and the Duchess of York, and the piety of the wailing women.

Tillyard's view of *King Richard III* as a 'moral history' related to the politics of Shakespeare's own time exercised a profound influence on scholars and students in the mid-twentieth century. But soon after his books were published, critics began to challenge his reading of the play. His views were criticised as being over-simplified, too influenced by his own assumptions, and by the need for national unity at the time he was writing (during the Second World War of 1939–45).

A P Rossiter's greatly admired essay in his book *Angel with Horns* (1961) challenges the simplicity of Tillyard's interpretation of the Tudor myth. Rossiter reveals the ambiguities and ironies implicit in the text and argues that the many ambiguities in the play make it more than part of the Tudor myth. Richard is morally evil, but he is also an attractive character, with his huge energy and dazzling wit. Rossiter argues that this paradox refutes the simplistic notion of 'good' overcoming 'evil', which is implicit in the Tudor myth. He concludes that this may be God's justice, 'but it sickens us': it is 'as pitiless as the Devil's'.

Rossiter ridicules the notion that the play in any way presents 'sober history' and also disagrees with Tillyard's interpretation of *King Richard III* as a moral history. A moral history (which may be interpreted as the working out of God's will on his people) implies a world that offers absolute certainties. Rossiter believes the ambiguities and ironies of the play were leading Shakespeare 'towards writing a comic history' rather than a tragedy. But he argues that *King Richard III* neither debunks nor disproves the Tudor myth.

Using a different approach, Caroline Spurgeon's book *Shakespeare's Imagery and What It Tells Us* (first published in 1935 and still in print) identifies 'image-clusters' as a dominant feature of the plays. Spurgeon counts the number of times such clusters occur and argues that they determine the distinctive atmosphere of a play. *King Richard III* contains recurring animal images that are linked to Richard, and also images of butcher and slaughterhouse. These clusters help to establish both the character of Richard and the play's preoccupation with death. Spurgeon also identifies the many references to trees and gardens that are often used to describe family and relationships within those families, particularly the family tree of the royal house. 'Thus the idea of trees, branches, plants and planting, ripeness, decay, weeds and flowers, "unblown" and withered, runs as an undertone throughout the play'.

The value of Caroline Spurgeon's pioneering study of Shakespeare's imagery has been acknowledged by later critics, but her work has also been much criticised. She rarely examines how the imagery relates to the dramatic context, claims that characters' opinions are Shakespeare's own, and that the imagery reveals the playwright's personality. A further criticism is that Spurgeon's tone is invariably one of praise, echoing the 'bardolatry' that has dogged Shakespeare criticism ever since the Romantics in the early nineteenth century. (For further examples of Spurgeon's study of imagery, see page 78.)

Modern criticism

Throughout the second half of the twentieth century and in the twenty-first, critical approaches to Shakespeare have radically challenged the traditional approaches described above. New critical approaches argue that traditional interpretations, with their focus on character, are too individualistic. Further, their detachment from the real world makes them elitist, sexist and apolitical.

Modern radical criticism asserts that traditional criticism divorces literary, dramatic and aesthetic matters from their social context. So modern criticism shifts from a focus on individuals to a concentration on social and material conditions. Traditional approaches are seen as concentrating on personal feelings and ignoring or simplifying history and society. They are criticised for taking a fatalistic view of human existence, for giving prominence to supernatural explanations, and implying that men and women are powerless to resist injustice, because despair and violence are inevitable. It seems fair to say that modern criticism seeks to give a much sharper edge to such approaches as those of Tillyard and Campbell.

Like traditional criticism, contemporary perspectives include many different approaches but share common features. Modern criticism:

- is sceptical of 'character' approaches (but often uses them!);
- concentrates on social, political and economic factors (arguing that these factors determine Shakespeare's creativity and audiences' and critics' interpretations);
- plays down or rejects supernatural and mysterious explanations;
- identifies contradictions, fragmentation and disunity in the plays;
- questions the possibility of 'happy' or 'hopeful' endings;
- produces readings that are subversive of existing social structures;
- identifies how the plays express the interests of dominant groups, most obviously, rich and powerful males;
- insists that 'theory' is essential to produce valid readings;
- often expresses its commitment to causes (for example, to feminism, or equality, or political change);
- argues that all readings are political or ideological readings (and that traditional criticism falsely claims to be objective).

Political criticism

The Richard Loncraine–Ian McKellen film of *Richard III* (1995) is set in the 1930s. The film opens with a tank bursting through the wall of a building containing Lancastrian supporters and ends with a battle scene in jeeps. Richmond corners Richard on the girders of a ruined factory. Richard reaches out with his 'good' hand and invites Richmond to join him. Richard overbalances and falls backwards to his death, Richmond shooting his pistol futilely after him. Richmond then smiles smugly at the camera as the song 'I'm Sitting On Top of the World' plays.

That this kind of adaptation can be made is due in some part to one of the earliest challengers of traditional criticism, the Polish critic Jan Kott. He fought with the Polish army and underground movement against the Nazis in the Second World War (1939–45), and had direct experience of the suffering and terror caused by Stalinist repression in Poland in the years after the war. Kott's book *Shakespeare Our Contemporary* draws parallels between the violence and cruelty of the modern world and the tyranny and despair that Shakespeare depicts in many of his plays.

Kott argues that history, rather than fate or the gods, is the cause of tragedy. He uses the image of 'the Grand Mechanism' of history: a great staircase up which characters, particularly the kings in the history plays, tread to their doom. Characters have little or no power over their lives and are swept aside by social and historical forces beyond their control. Kott describes the beginning of *King Richard III* in this context. Henry VI and Clarence have been murdered and Edward IV has died. 'There is only Richard and the steps he has yet to climb on the way to the throne. Each of these steps is a living man'. He points out the inexorable nature of the process:

> There are no gods in Shakespeare. There are only kings, every one of whom is an executioner and victim in turn. There are also living, frightened people.

Kott praises the way in which Shakespeare portrays ordinary people in brief, revealing scenes when tragedy is projected onto an everyday level. Crimes are legalised by people like the Scrivener. A servant knocks on Hastings' door at four o'clock in the morning, unaware that he is part of a chain of events that will end in Hastings' death. Kott's own background under Stalinist rule is vividly revealed by his attitude towards this episode. The director Peter Brook comments that Jan Kott 'is undoubtedly the only writer on Elizabethan matters who assumes without question that every one of his readers will at some point have been woken by the police in the middle of the night'.

Kott describes the end of a performance that he greatly admired. It opened with iron bars being lowered to form a background. Richard is played as a 'buffoon' with a frightening laugh. At the end of the play, the new king talks of peace, forgiveness and justice and then suddenly makes a crowing sound of laughter just like Richard's, and the bars start to be lowered again.

The buffoon Kott described became a jester dressed in traditional costume in the Royal Shakespeare Company's 1995 production, but a jester with a psychotic personality. The video (1990) from the English Shakespeare Company (see Resources, page 128) also reflects Kott's influence. Richard looks anything but a king. Dressed in a smart, pinstriped suit and bald-headed, his physical disabilities are suggested by a single leather glove. Buckingham slyly and intelligently explains away Richard's brutal actions like a modern-day spin-doctor.

Kott has been much criticised by later critics because, for all his insistence on social context, he focuses on the individual as a tragic hero more than as a product of society and the time. But Kott still exercises a powerful influence. He can be seen as the forerunner of new critical ideas that focus on the social and political contexts and causes of tragedy. His bleak view of history has informed understanding of *King Richard III* as a play about *realpolitik* (see page 61) by linking brutal struggles for power in Shakespeare's time with those seen in the present day.

In the closing decades of the twentieth century two major schools of political criticism emerged: new historicism (largely American) and cultural materialism (largely British). Their assumptions are virtually the same, but cultural materialism is more concerned with today's world, whereas new historicism focuses on the Elizabethan and Jacobean periods.

For most students, it is probably best not to attempt to pigeonhole the different types of political criticism. It is more helpful to think of them as sharing a way of reading plays which argues that culture (e.g. drama) and materialism (e.g. economic factors) are always related. Interpretations are shaped by the economic, political and ideological systems of the times.

Jonathan Dollimore, in his influential book *Radical Tragedy* (second edition 1989), rejects the ideas of the traditional critics, arguing that criticism should centre upon society. He believes that many of the plays written by Elizabethan and Jacobean dramatists actively question and subvert contemporary political power and ideology. They expose the injustices and inequalities of their society and question the beliefs and structures that maintain those unfair practices.

Dollimore argues that society was disunited on many of the great issues of the day and there was passionate contemporary debate and argument about the place of history and religion in contemporary life. He therefore attacks Tillyard's view of the Elizabethan world picture and the Tudor myth as being 'discredited by new criticism'. Dollimore argues that there was not one but many versions of the myth. 'The monarch was seen either as agent or transgressor of God's plan'. Whether the monarch was an 'agent' or 'transgressor' depended on the bias of the historian (Lancastrian or Yorkist). The myth would not unite an audience, but would reveal to them how such myths can be ideologically exploited.

Dollimore also attacks traditional 'character' criticism, asserting that human personality is determined by and reflects the conditions of the time. It is not stable or unified, but full of contradictions. Richard is an example. 'The amoral individualist' of the drama possesses not a fixed identity, but a chameleon one, 'subtle, false, and treacherous' (Act 1 Scene 1, line 37). Richard can no longer define himself as he awakes from his nightmare before the Battle of Bosworth. Dollimore describes this as follows: 'at the point when power is slipping from him, an attempt to reassert autonomy collapses into paradoxical self-division' (Act 5 Scene 3, lines 182–91).

Graham Holderness in *Shakespeare: The Histories* points out that the history plays (including *King Richard III*) were written looking back to a time of chivalric antiquity, epic heroism and masculine virtue. This past age was clearly different from contemporary (Elizabethan) times. These old values of war, dominant figures of masculine heroism and military enterprise were relatively marginal to the central priorities of the late Tudor state. A violent world dominated by male rulers empowered by feudal and chivalric values was not the world of Shakespeare. Holderness argues that the world of Richard III was totally different to Shakespeare's England of 'the female monarch and sober-suited civil servants who presided over a civilised and peaceful culture'.

Much of Holderness' criticism focuses on Richard as a symbol of those contradictory ideas. Richard's opening soliloquy shows him as a supporter of war in a time of peace 'inhibited by a luckless combination of heredity and environment that has stranded a deformed and violent soldier in an oppressive time of tranquil normality'. Richard feels trapped in the wrong time, but also haunted by figures and deeds from the past. He has believed himself to be fully in control of his environment. He has forced his will on the present with his ruthless actions. He has retold the past in his own interpretations (for example, the death of Rutland). He has also manipulated historical records to show his own version of the future, as in having the Scrivener rewrite Hastings' indictment. But he has not succeeded in his aims, showing that, in Holderness' words, 'men both make and mistake their own history'.

Feminist criticism

Feminism aims to achieve rights and equality for women in social, political and economic life. It challenges sexism: those beliefs that result in the degradation, oppression and subordination of women. Feminist criticism challenges traditional portrayals of women characters. It rejects 'male ownership' of criticism, in which men determined what questions were to be asked of a play, and which answers were acceptable. *King Richard III* may seem to have powerful appeal to feminist critics because the women appear as victims, used and humiliated by men.

In an early feminist essay, 'The Paradox of Power in *Richard III*' (1981), Irene G Dash explores the powerlessness of the women who are married to men of power, but who change their attitudes to males by the end of the play. At first the women are angry, irrational, self-doubting, self-denigrating and, ultimately, denigrating of all women. This does not fully apply to Margaret, whose first appearance comes as 'a welcome antidote to Richard's swaggering triumph with Anne' because she is unafraid. Margaret curses everyone, but especially Elizabeth, because she has stolen Margaret's position as queen. To Dash, this reveals that 'she is still a victim of that minority-status psychology that mandates she express her deepest contempt for another woman'.

In Act 4 Scene 4 the women discover solidarity and strength. Margaret no longer needs to curse, for her curses have come true and she can return to France. Now, for the first time, the women speak as equals and show mutual support towards each other. Margaret has given the Duchess and Elizabeth strength by teaching them to remember the past and how to curse. Elizabeth and the Duchess now have the will to stand up to Richard. The Duchess prays for his death at the hands of his enemies. Elizabeth foils Richard's plot to consolidate his position as king by failing to comply with his plans for marrying her daughter. Dash concludes that the play 'reveals the limited world that exists as long as people believe that power belongs to men and powerlessness to women'.

Juliet Dusinberre, in *Shakespeare and the Nature of Women*, claims that 'Shakespeare's feminism lies in his scepticism about the nature of women'. She argues that Shakespeare challenged Elizabethan preconceptions about women. His audiences would have felt women's influence sharply and debated attitudes towards them keenly:

Shakespeare saw men and women as equal in a world which declared them as unequal. He observed in the individual woman or man an infinite variety of union between opposing impulses . . . he refused to separate their worlds physically, intellectually or spiritually.

Dusinberre's book examines the changing role of women and gender relationships in late Elizabethan society. She argues that 'Shakespeare's theatre offers a consistent probing of the reactions of women to isolation in a society which has never allowed them independence from men, either physically or spiritually'. As an example, Dusinberre quotes Anne's and Jane Shore's isolation in the play.

Dusinberre views Richard's seduction of Anne as a 'calculated experiment in courtly love'. Anne's pity for Richard excites not the gratitude of the courtly lover, but his scorn. Richard's cynical wooing therefore turns the traditional courtly lover, with his idolatry of the woman he woos, into satire. Satirising women was the function of the Vice in the morality plays (see page 65), and was a traditional subject of drama. The character of Anne could remind an audience of that tradition, but it would also be aware of the weakness of a woman who is isolated from society by the death of those men nearest to her.

Dusinberre argues that witches and whores used their arts for personal gain and empowerment. Jane Shore is accused of being both witch and whore, and Richard, in a theatrical passion, successfully accuses her of being responsible for his deformity because of her arts. Richard uses Shore's own most potent weapons against her, but in doing so reveals the double standards of a society that allows men to use women as they wish.

Phyllis Rackin bases her analysis of the play upon its genre: history or tragedy. She argues in *History into Tragedy: The Case of Richard III* that 'Shakespeare shifts from the loose chronicle form of the early histories to the tightly focused structure of tragedy that restricted the range of possible roles for women. They gain in sympathetic portrayal, but lose power.' She states that the male claims centre stage, with soliloquies which give him 'privileged subjectivity'. The play finishes as it starts, with speeches from male characters. She relates this to the emergence of a capitalist economy and nation-state 'that increasingly employed the mystified image of a patriarchal family to authorise masculine privilege and rationalise monarchical power'. Richmond can only gain legality as king through Princess Elizabeth's 'genealogical authority', but she never appears in the play. Rackin is particularly alert to the disempowering of Margaret, who changes from the 'adulterous wife and bloodthirsty warrior' of the previous *King Henry VI* history plays, to the 'bereaved and suffering prophet'.

Feminist criticism has greatly extended ways of understanding *King Richard III*. As such, it challenges theatrical practice in which it has been common to cut the role of Margaret severely or entirely from the play, greatly reduce the lines of the Duchess and Elizabeth (especially in Act 4 Scene 4) and cut lines from Richard and Anne's long wooing scene. Feminist criticism has successfully demonstrated that these women's roles are essential to Shakespeare's argument. They are crucial voices that proclaim Richard's hellish genesis and evil crimes in a cowed state.

Performance criticism: the afterlife of *King Richard III*

Performance criticism is concerned with the staging of the play in the theatre or on film and video. It is part of what is often called the 'afterlife' of *King Richard III*: what happens to the play after the author has written it. Such criticism vividly reveals the instability of *King Richard III*. The play takes very different forms in its afterlife, performed and received very differently at different times. The instability begins with the existence of nine different versions of the play, the eight Quartos and the Folio (see pages 74–5). It is heightened by the way in which directors and actors have created new performances of the play over the centuries. Performance criticism therefore fully acknowledges that *King Richard III* is a play: a script to be performed by actors. As such, performance critics note how much *King Richard III* uses the language of theatre: 'induction', 'play', 'part' and other dramatic terms. They identify how the concepts of drama are integral to the play (see page 68).

King Richard III has always been among the most popular of Shakespeare's plays, and the part of Richard is an opportunity for virtuoso acting. The image of a physically misshapen and morally corrupt king has inspired a vast number of spin-offs from the eighteenth century onwards. Modern offshoots and adaptations include films, paintings, cartoons, novels and numerous parodies. The actor Antony Sher, himself a famous Richard, remarked that 'A horse! a horse! my kingdom for a horse!' is probably the second most famous line in the whole of Shakespeare, second only to 'To be, or not to be'.

Richard Burbage, one of the greatest actors of the Elizabethan age, was the first Richard. The stories, allusions and parodies that remain from Shakespeare's time are enough to suggest that both the play and its star were very popular. That popularity was evident at Burbage's funeral in 1619, recorded in a lament written to honour the great actor. It mourned that 'Crookback, as befits, shall cease to live'.

But performances of *King Richard III* declined as momentous historical events outshone even Richard's dazzling evil: Charles I was beheaded; England plunged into civil war and the new puritan government closed all theatres between 1642 and 1660.

Burbage and successive actors had used versions of Shakespeare's text from the first performances until 1699. The dramatist, actor and Poet Laureate Colley Cibber (1671–1757) published a new and radical adaptation in 1700, which aimed to restore the popularity of the play. Cibber's new version was so acclaimed that it remained the preferred acting text until the closing decades of the nineteenth century. It continued its influence into the twentieth century, and even the 1955 film version by Laurence Olivier retains many of Cibber's changes.

What were Cibber's alterations? He cut the play by almost half its original length, retaining only about 800 of Shakespeare's lines and splicing in parts from Shakespeare's other history plays. He also added about 1,000 lines of his own. The part of Richard was enlarged to account for more than 40 per cent of the play instead of the third given by Shakespeare. Cibber's version focuses relentlessly on Richard, his feelings and those of his victims. He cut the parts of Margaret, Clarence, Hastings and King Edward. Eight scenes were deleted, and the roles of Buckingham, Rivers, Grey and Vaughan reduced in importance.

The Cibber version had important consequences for early critical approaches. It is essential to distinguish between the critics who write about a performance (for they will almost certainly be referring to the Cibber adaptation) and the critics who write about what they have read (where the text is almost certainly by Shakespeare, as represented in the Quartos or Folio). This difference between reading the plays as written by Shakespeare and seeing them in Cibber's adaptation continued until late into the nineteenth century. Two early writers on

King Richard III, George Steevens and Charles Lamb, vividly illustrate this conflict between what might be called the 'page' version and the 'stage' version.

George Steevens was an early critic of the play, who admired Cibber's stage version but not Shakespeare's original text. In 1793, commenting first on Shakespeare's original version, he writes 'I most cordially join with Dr Johnson and Mr Malone in their opinions that *Richard III* was over-valued'. He then comments on Cibber's version that the 'part of Richard is perhaps above all others variegated' (has a great deal of variety) and adds that it is only well received now because of Mr Cibber's 'judicious reformation'. He lists all the parts omitted by Cibber that he calls 'undramatik incumberances' and which the play is better off without.

Charles Lamb disagreed. Lamb was a writer who admired Shakespeare and retold the plots of the plays in an edition for children called *Lamb's Tales from Shakespeare* (actually mainly written by his sister, Mary). Writing in 1801, he makes a clear distinction between 'the wretched *Acting* [his italics] play of that name, which you will see altered by Cibber' and Shakespeare's original: 'I am possessed with an Admiration of the genuine Richard'. He praises the ambivalence of Shakespeare's Richard compared to Cibber's, and declares that Shakespeare 'set out to paint a monster, but his human sympathies produced a Man'.

A year later Lamb wrote in praise of Richard's humour 'the quality of unrestrained mirth' that he believed was the 'prime feature of his character'. He also admires Richard's 'most exquisite address' to Queen Elizabeth as 'the most finished piece of eloquence in the world'. Lamb was clearly reading the play in Shakespeare's version, as Cibber destroys that 'eloquence' because he added lines in which Elizabeth tells the audience she has no intention of letting Richard marry her daughter!

The play has always been a star vehicle for the leading actors of each generation, and each era creates its own version and interpretation. Many great actors have portrayed Richard, but one eighteenth-century and one nineteenth-century production are landmarks.

David Garrick made his debut as Richard in 1741 using the Cibber version, and performed the role 213 times between 1747 and 1776. Garrick's Richard was a triumph. The mobility of his face and flexibility of gesture for which he was famous attempted to fuse both mind and action into a naturalistic style, providing a sharp contrast to the artificial theatricality of past performers. William Hogarth's picture *David Garrick as Richard III* (1745) is a frozen moment from that famous portrayal. It hangs in the Walker Art Gallery in Liverpool, and most editions of the play contain a reproduction of the painting. Richard wakes in his very elaborate tent at Bosworth, one hand grasping his sword and the other held palm outward, fingers stretched in terror. The objects he has dishonoured, the crown and garter, surround him, and behind him is a picture of Christ crucified. His armour lies on the floor and the tents and fires of his troops are painted onto the backcloth behind the tent.

More than a century after Garrick, Henry Irving, the famous actor–manager, experienced a great theatrical triumph in his 1877 production. He restored much of Shakespeare's original text, retaining two-thirds of Shakespeare's lines, but cutting the historical references and some of the other characters. He played Richard with 'youthful audacity'. Nineteen years later he again played Richard to great acclaim, but the production reflected the older Irving. He had 'outlived all pleasures but the intellectual one of doing evil superbly'. It was this production that reinstated Margaret's role as crucial to the drama.

Twentieth-century productions have increasingly emphasised the play as a political allegory, reflecting the rise of fascism and the totalitarian state. A famous 1920 production at the Berlin Schauspielhaus greatly influenced Jan Kott in his theory of the 'Grand Mechanism' (see page 93). The second half of the production was dominated by a huge red staircase that Richard climbed, only to tumble from the top at the end of the play.

Some productions question the very nature of the play. The Polish actor Jacek Woszczerowicz played Richard's role using his skills as a comic actor. The notion of combining the political with the humorous was strikingly realised by Ramaz Chkhivadze in a Georgian expressionist production in 1980. It was performed in the Georgian language as a symbolic political allegory. In performances outside Georgia, few people could understand the language, but Antony Sher describes its power, as Richard was played 'like a species of giant poisonous toad'. There was a manic humour about the production. At the moment Richard was proclaimed king, the crown 'seemed to squash the face beneath it, like an animated cartoon'.

Sher's own Richard for the Royal Shakespeare Company in 1984 was a hugely athletic, physical performance. He used two crutches and gave the appearance of a huge spider. Sher's book *The Year of the King* gives a fascinating account of the various ideas that went into the creating of his Richard. These included the mass murderer Dennis Nilsen; a TV programme called *Inside the Third Reich*; a work centre for the physically disabled; a study of hunchbacks; thoughts about the Antichrist and Jung's 'modern man in search of a soul'; and a woman who believed 'Richard III is the sexiest [character] of them all'.

The widespread availability of films of *King Richard III* on video and DVD has made performance criticism even more significant in the twenty-first century. Film offers valuable opportunities to analyse aspects of performance in different productions: character, relationships, conceptual and interpretive approaches, cuts and settings. Film also provides close-ups, tracking shots and cinematic spectacle not available on stage. In Olivier's film, the crown is trampled in the mud before Richard is stabbed to death and his body thrown over a horse. His misshapen shadow is cast over many scenes, and Olivier's speeches directly to the camera leave no doubt of his evil intent.

Olivier's film was set in medieval England, but the McKellen–Loncraine film is much less traditional, being set in the 1930s. The period enabled Loncraine to use the film conventions of the time, such as Hollywood musicals, the gangster film, war films and the action–adventure movie.

Al Pacino's 1996 film *Looking for Richard* tries to discover what Shakespeare means at the end of the twentieth century. Filmed extracts from the play and from rehearsals are intercut with discussions with actors and academics and combined with *cinéma-vérité* (documentary style) interviews with people in the streets. Pacino's direction of *King Richard III* echoes gangster movies, particularly *The Godfather*.

Psychoanalytic criticism

In the twentieth century, psychoanalysis became a major influence on the understanding and interpretation of human behaviour. The founder of psychoanalysis, Sigmund Freud, explained personality as the result of unconscious and irrational desires, repressed memories or wishes, sexuality, fantasy, anxiety and conflict. Freud's theories, together with his stress on early childhood experiences, have a strong influence on criticism and stagings of Shakespeare's plays. Freud regards Richard as an example of a person who is conscious from infancy of an 'unjust disadvantage'. Freud argues that Richard's predicament allows the audience to have 'a secret background of sympathy' for him, because he expresses 'an enormous magnification of something we find in ourselves as well . . . we all demand reparation for early wounds to our narcissism, our self-love'.

King Richard III has attracted comparatively little psychoanalytic criticism. Norman Holland comments that because of the scattered nature of such criticism 'it is difficult to piece together a coherent psychoanalytic picture of the play'. Nonetheless, Holland's book, *Psychoanalysis and Shakespeare*, shows how psychoanalytic interpretations of *King Richard III* eroticise politics, seeking sexual or unconscious motives in the play. Here are some features of such interpretations:

- the pervasiveness of incest motives (Richard has killed Anne's fiancé and father, and by marrying her becomes her husband and father)
- the notion that Stanley's leaving his son as hostage reveals his secret hostility towards the child
- the view of Richard as a 'spurned child', rejected by his mother, who therefore strives to outdo his brothers
- Richard's unconscious fear of women. He sublimates his sexual desire, turning it into a desire for power
- the idea that Richard's physical deformity leads to an inferiority complex and a compensatory reaction: a superiority complex
- the view of Clarence's dream as a 'punishment dream' in which his conscience (superego) tortures him
- England's civil strife being described at the end of the play as incest killings:

> England hath long been mad, and scarred herself;
> The brother blindly shed the brother's blood;
> The father rashly slaughtered his own son;
> The son, compelled, been butcher to the sire
>
> *(Act 5 Scene 5, lines 23–6)*

Such interpretations reveal the obvious weaknesses in applying psychoanalytic theories to *King Richard III*. They cannot be proved or disproved, they neglect historical, political and social factors that are fundamental to the play, and they are highly speculative. When applied to drama, psychoanalytic approaches often impose meaning from theory rather than Shakespeare's text. Nonetheless, because psychoanalysis is concerned with personal trauma or anxiety and with dysfunctional family relationships, *King Richard III* has obvious features that invite psychoanalytic approaches: a chief protagonist perfect for the psychoanalyst's couch; dysfunctional family relationships; profound guilt; dreams and ghosts. But the most helpful psychoanalytic criticism like Marjorie Garber's essay 'Descanting on Deformity' attempts to incorporate the insights of psychoanalysis into a discussion that considers historical and social factors.

Postmodern criticism

Postmodern criticism (sometimes called 'deconstruction') is not always easy to understand because it is not centrally concerned with consistency or reasoned argument. It does not accept that one section of the story is necessarily connected to what follows, or that characters relate to each other in meaningful ways. The approach therefore has obvious drawbacks in providing a model for examination students who are expected to display consistency and reasoned argument.

Postmodern approaches to *King Richard III* are most clearly seen in stage productions or films. There, you could think of it simply as a mixture of styles. The label 'postmodern' is applied to productions that self-consciously show little regard for consistency in character or for coherence in telling the story. Characters are dressed in costumes from very different historical periods, and carry both ancient and modern weapons.

A telling example of such inconsistency is the Royal National Theatre production of 1989, in which Ian McKellen played Richard (and which later proved the inspiration for the 1995 film). Richard changed into a variety of different costumes throughout the play. He began in a First World War greatcoat, changed into an Elizabethan doublet and hose for the coronation and ended wearing medieval armour for the final duel with Richmond.

Shakespeare himself has been regarded as a postmodern writer in the way he mixes genres. *King Richard III* is a history, chronicle and tragedy, but is also a comedy. Shakespeare commonly mixes genres within scenes, for example the grotesquely comic murderers who discuss money and conscience before killing Clarence (Act 1 Scene 4); the farcical manner in which Richard gains the throne (Act 3 Scenes 5 and 7).

A more complicated aspect of postmodern theory asserts that human beings have no essential identity. Jonathan Dollimore argues that historical and social forces shape characters in plays, like those in real life. Deconstructionists interpret Richard's speech as he wakes from his nightmare before the Battle of Bosworth as a demonstration of his 'disintegrated identity'.

Deconstruction frequently claims to show that what is really going on in a play often challenges traditional readings. Many political, feminist and psychoanalytic interpretations are sometimes claimed as being examples of deconstruction because of the strong reactions that they provoke. Some varieties of deconstruction, particularly concerned with language, claim that it is impossible to find meaning in language as words simply refer to other words, and so any interpretation is endlessly delayed (or 'deferred' as the deconstructionists say). Other critics focus on minor or marginal characters, or gaps or silences in the play. They claim that these features, previously overlooked as unimportant, reveal significant truths about the play. Because of such assumptions, postmodern criticism is sometimes described as 'reading against the grain' or less politely as 'textual harassment'. The approaches are certainly exciting and imaginative, but it must again be stated that their lack of concern for rational argument and coherent meaning make them unhelpful approaches for all but the most confident examination student.

Organising your responses

The purpose of this section is to help you improve your writing about *King Richard III*. It offers practical guidance on two kinds of tasks: writing about an extract from the play and writing an essay. Whether you are answering an examination question, preparing coursework (term papers) or carrying out research on your chosen topic, this section will help you organise and present your responses.

In all your writing, there are three vital things to remember:

- *King Richard III* is a play. Although it is usually referred to as a 'text', *King Richard III* is not a book, but a script intended to be acted on a stage. So your writing should demonstrate an awareness of the play in performance as theatre. That means you should always try to read the play with an 'inner eye', thinking about how it could look and sound on stage. By doing so, you will be able to write effectively about Shakespeare's language and dramatic techniques.

- *King Richard III* is not a presentation of 'reality'. It is a dramatic construct in which the playwright, through theatre, engages the emotions and intellect of the audience. The characters and story may persuade an audience to suspend its disbelief for several hours. The audience may identify with the characters, be deeply moved by them, and may think of them as if they are living human beings. However, when you write, a major part of your task is to show how Shakespeare achieves the dramatic effects that so engage the audience. Through discussion of his handling of language, character and plot, your writing reveals how Shakespeare uses themes and ideas, attitudes and values, to give insight into crucial social, moral and political dilemmas of his time – and yours.

- How Shakespeare learned his craft. As a schoolboy, and in his early years as a dramatist, Shakespeare used all kinds of models or frameworks to guide his writing. But he quickly learned how to vary and adapt the models to his own dramatic purposes. This section offers frameworks that you can use to structure your writing. As you use them, follow Shakespeare's example! Adapt them to suit your own writing style and needs.

Writing about an extract

It is an expected part of all Shakespeare study that you should be able to write well about an extract (sometimes called a 'passage') from the play. An extract is usually between 30 and 70 lines long, and you are invited to comment on it. The instructions vary. Sometimes the task is very briefly expressed:

- Write a detailed commentary on the following passage.
  or
- Write about the effect of the extract on your own thoughts and feelings.

At other times a particular focus is specified for your writing:

- With close reference to the language and imagery of the passage, show in what ways it helps to establish important issues in the play.
  or
- Analyse the style and structure of the extract, showing what it contributes to the play's major concerns.

In writing your response, you must of course take account of the precise wording of the task, and ensure you concentrate on each particular point specified. But however the invitation to write about an extract is expressed, it requires you to comment in detail on the language. You should identify and evaluate how the language reveals character, contributes to plot development, offers opportunities for dramatic effect, and embodies crucial concerns of the play as a whole. These 'crucial concerns' are also referred to as the 'themes', or 'issues', or 'preoccupations' of the play.

The framework on page 109 is a guide to how you can write a detailed commentary on an extract. Writing a paragraph on each item will help you bring out the meaning and significance of the extract, and show how Shakespeare achieves his effects.

> **Paragraph 1:** Locate the extract in the play and say who is on stage.
> **Paragraph 2:** State what the extract is about and identify its structure.
> **Paragraph 3:** Identify the mood or atmosphere of the extract.
> **Paragraphs 4–8:**
> Diction (vocabulary)
> Imagery
> Antithesis
> Repetition
> Lists
> } These paragraphs analyse how Shakespeare achieves his effects. They concentrate on the language of the extract, showing the dramatic effect of each item, and how the language expresses crucial concerns of the play.
> **Paragraph 9:** Staging opportunities
> **Paragraph 10:** Conclusion

The following example uses the framework to show how the paragraphs making up the essay might be written. The framework headings (in bold) would not, of course, appear in your essay. They are presented only to help you see how the framework is used.

Extract

RICHARD   Now is the winter of our discontent
        Made glorious summer by this son of York,
        And all the clouds that loured upon our house
        In the deep bosom of the ocean buried.
        Now are our brows bound with victorious wreaths,   5
        Our bruisèd arms hung up for monuments,
        Our stern alarums changed to merry meetings,
        Our dreadful marches to delightful measures.
        Grim-visaged war hath smoothed his wrinkled front,
        And now, instead of mounting barbèd steeds   10
        To fright the souls of fearful adversaries,
        He capers nimbly in a lady's chamber
        To the lascivious pleasing of a lute.
        But I that am not shaped for sportive tricks
        Nor made to court an amorous looking-glass,   15
        I that am rudely stamped and want love's majesty
        To strut before a wanton ambling nymph,
        I that am curtailed of this fair proportion,
        Cheated of feature by dissembling nature,
        Deformed, unfinished, sent before my time   20

Into this breathing world scarce half made up,
And that so lamely and unfashionable
That dogs bark at me as I halt by them,
Why, I in this weak piping time of peace,
Have no delight to pass away the time,   25
Unless to see my shadow in the sun
And descant on mine own deformity.
And therefore, since I cannot prove a lover
To entertain these fair well-spoken days,
I am determinèd to prove a villain   30
And hate the idle pleasures of these days.
Plots have I laid, inductions dangerous,
By drunken prophecies, libels, and dreams
To set my brother Clarence and the king
In deadly hate the one against the other.   35
And if King Edward be as true and just
As I am subtle, false, and treacherous,
This day should Clarence closely be mewed up
About a prophecy which says that 'G'
Of Edward's heirs the murderer shall be.   40
Dive, thoughts, down to my soul, here Clarence comes.

Enter CLARENCE *guarded by* BRAKENBURY

Brother, good day. What means this armèd guard
That waits upon your grace?
CLARENCE   His majesty,
Tend'ring my person's safety, hath appointed
This conduct to convey me to the Tower.   45
RICHARD   Upon what cause?
CLARENCE   Because my name is George.
RICHARD   Alack, my lord, that fault is none of yours.
He should for that commit your godfathers.
Oh, belike his majesty hath some intent
That you should be new christened in the Tower.   50
But what's the matter, Clarence? May I know?
CLARENCE   Yea, Richard, when I know, but I protest
As yet I do not. But as I can learn,
He hearkens after prophecies and dreams,
And from the cross-row plucks the letter 'G',   55

And says a wizard told him that by 'G'
His issue disinherited should be.
And for my name of George begins with 'G',
It follows in his thought that I am he.
These, as I learn, and suchlike toys as these   60
Hath moved his highness to commit me now.
RICHARD   Why, this it is when men are ruled by women.
'Tis not the king that sends you to the Tower.
My lady Grey, his wife, Clarence, 'tis she
That tempts him to this harsh extremity.   65
Was it not she and that good man of worship,
Anthony Woodville, her brother there,
That made him send Lord Hastings to the Tower,
From whence this present day he is delivered?
We are not safe, Clarence, we are not safe.   70

(Act 1 Scene 1, lines 1–70)

Paragraph 1: Locate the extract in the play and say who is on stage.

The house of York has seized power following a bitter civil war, and
England is at peace under the rule of Richard's brother, King Edward
IV. In his soliloquy that opens the play, Richard shares with the
audience his dislike of the present time and reveals his bloody future
plans. Part of those plans involves his brother, Clarence. The two
brothers meet briefly on stage, watched by the silent Brakenbury.

After the extract, Hastings' release from the Tower at the moment
Clarence is escorted into it stresses England's political instability. The
scene ends as Richard resumes his interrupted soliloquy, confiding to
the audience his hopes that King Edward will not die until Clarence
has been executed. He will then marry Anne Neville.

Paragraph 2: State what the extract is about and identify its structure.

(Begin with one or two sentences identifying what the extract is about,
followed by several sentences briefly identifying its structure, that is,
the different sections of the extract.)

The soliloquy immediately establishes Richard as a villain, who
attempts to seduce the audience into accepting his evil plans through
his charm and wit. The trusting Clarence is unaware that Richard is
responsible for his imprisonment, as Richard pretends sympathy for
him and blames others. Structurally, the soliloquy establishes

dramatic irony for the scene that follows. The audience can enjoy Richard's performance as the sympathetic brother who first feigns surprise at Clarence's imprisonment, and then blames Queen Elizabeth and her brother for both Clarence's and Hastings' predicaments. Finally, Richard hypocritically suggests that they are all at risk from the queen and her family's plotting.

Paragraph 3: Identify the mood or atmosphere of the extract.
Richard's opening words swiftly establish the mood of mocking irony that will characterise the whole extract. Richard demonstrates his brilliant wit, huge energy and charismatic personality which he will later use to ceaselessly ridicule, insult, taunt and deceive all who stand in his way to power. His soliloquy reveals that he is a self-proclaimed villain who is isolated by choice, and these qualities swiftly create an atmosphere of deceit and distrust as he speaks with Clarence. His double-edged words contain ominous meanings for Clarence and create chilling humour as he shares his cleverness with the audience.

Paragraph 4: Diction
Richard's soliloquy reveals his delight in language and wordplay. He ridicules and derides the present time by contrasting war with peace ('winter'/'summer'; 'marches'/'measures'; 'mounting barbèd steeds' / 'capers nimbly'; 'clouds'/'ocean'). The contrasting diction continues as he compares himself to Edward ('amorous'/'sportive tricks'; 'Deformed'/'fair proportion'). His mocking tone is reflected in the sounds of his words: there is assonance ('clouds', 'loured', 'our house') and alliteration ('brows bound' and 'merry meetings'). He puns on the different meanings of 'son'/'sun' and 'curtailed'. He is 'determinèd' to be a villain (meaning he is 'resolved' but also with an opposite meaning: 'decreed beforehand by God'). 'Plots' and 'inductions' remind the audience of Richard's love of acting. Clarence's vocabulary in contrast appears naive and uncomplicated. He retells the prophecy in simple rhyme with the repetition of 'G' that contrasts with Richard's double-edged replies. Richard frequently uses words that state one thing but imply another to create situations rich in dramatic irony. He does not want Clarence to have a 'good day' and knows all the answers to his questions before he asks them. Richard's words reveal contempt for Queen Elizabeth ('ruled by women'; 'My lady Grey, his wife').

Paragraph 5: Imagery

Richard's antagonism towards his crowned brother and the period of peace is established through imagery. The 'winter of our discontent' has given way to the 'glorious summer' of Yorkist rule, but Richard is associated with winter, for he hates the son/sun of Edward. The sun (the emblem of the house of York) becomes a metaphor for King Edward, whose handsome figure contrasts so powerfully with his brother's twisted features. Richard's only use for the sun is to see his own shadow and play a variety of ingenious variations ('descant') on the theme of his 'own deformity'. Richard associates his birth and body with a dog (in Elizabethan times 'curtailed' was associated with clipping off the tails of animals) and begins the animal images that will reinforce his predatory nature throughout the play. That rapacious nature is quickly revealed, for Richard is responsible for Clarence being 'mewed up' (imprisoned like a bird of prey).

Richard's hatred of peace is forcefully expressed as he personifies the clouds that frowned ('loured') and that are now consigned to the 'bosom of the ocean'. Richard mocks his brother Edward, personifying war as a soldier who has exchanged his martial aspects, including his scowl ('Grim-visaged'), for those of a lover.

Paragraph 6: Antithesis

Richard's contrariness is revealed in all kinds of oppositions. The contrasts between war and peace are expressed in antithetical phrases: 'stern alarums' are transformed into 'merry meetings' and 'dreadful marches' to 'delightful measures'. The bedroom replaces the battlefield as King Edward mounts not 'barbèd steeds' (horses covered in armour) but his mistress. Richard cannot be a 'lover' so he will prove 'a villain'. Edward is as 'true and just' as Richard is 'subtle, false, and treacherous'. Men being ruled by women cause the present troubles. Clarence is imprisoned as Hastings gains his freedom.

Paragraph 7: Repetition

Richard repeats the pronoun 'our' six times in the opening 13 lines to distance himself from present events and stress his isolation. 'But I that am not shaped for sportive tricks' signals Richard's change to the personal pronoun; 'I' occurs nine times between this point and the entry of Clarence as he shares his private thoughts with the audience. The contrast of past wars and present peace is emphasised by the repetition of 'now' and 'these days'. Richard's repetition of 'We are not safe' stresses the ironic humour of the episode, for Clarence mistrusts all except his own brother, and by 'We' Richard really means 'you'.

Paragraph 8: Lists
Shakespeare uses another language technique to enable Richard to express his disenchantment with the present time. He lists what causes Richard's feelings, piling up item on item to heighten the impact of his words. Richard's catalogue of contrasting images of war and peace swiftly establish his contrary nature. His outward appearance reads like a grotesque inventory ('not shaped'; 'rudely stamped'; 'Cheated of feature'; 'Deformed, unfinished'; 'lamely and unfashionable'; 'dogs bark at me'; 'halt'; 'deformity'). Richard lists the techniques he will use against Clarence ('Plots', 'inductions', 'prophecies, libels, and dreams'). Edward is 'true and just' but Richard is 'subtle, false, and treacherous'.

Paragraph 9: Staging opportunities
Many productions attempt to establish the play's atmosphere and concerns in the opening moments through a striking dramatic image. Ian McKellen's film begins with an eight-minute sequence that includes a battle followed by Yorkist celebrations (before Richard even speaks). On stage, one production had Richard speak his opening soliloquy through a snowstorm to reinforce his wintry disposition. Elizabethan audiences would recognise Richard as the medieval morality figure of the Vice, whose charm, wit and double-dealing would trap the unwary into sin. This grotesquely smiling figure, grasping for his dagger as he jokes and shares his schemes, would both repel and entertain Elizabethans. Today, some directors continue that tradition by emphasising Richard's grotesque appearance, playing up his humour as he delights in fooling his enemies. But many modern productions seek to link the play to *realpolitik*, presenting Richard as a smooth-talking, plausible character who successfully hides his real brutality behind clever spin and presentation. Such productions only hint at Richard's deformity. Actors have portrayed Richard as jester, buffoon, military commander and comedian. All attempt, by addressing the audience directly as confidants, to convince them of Richard's intelligence, wit, charisma and delight in acting a part. Clarence's entrance allows Richard to

demonstrate those formidable skills as he pretends sympathy for his brother. Brakenbury's silence is often presented on stage as an example of the powerlessness of ordinary citizens.

Paragraph 10: Conclusion
The opening scene offers many opportunities for different ways of performance. It is crucial to establish the director's conception of the play and interpretation of Richard's character from the opening soliloquy. Richard must quickly establish his complex character that is so at odds with the present time, for this will provide the dramatic conflict for the scenes that follow. Richard's soliloquy begins the irony and dramatic irony that pervades the play, and establishes the mocking, contemptuous tone as Richard confidently exercises his superiority over others. That superiority is demonstrated in the brief scene with Clarence, where Shakespeare emphasises the ominous yet grotesquely humorous nature of Richard's intrigue and plotting.

Reminders
- Structure your response in paragraphs. Each paragraph makes a particular point and helps build up your argument.
- Focus tightly on the language, especially vocabulary, imagery, antithesis, lists, repetitions.
- Remember that *King Richard III* is a play. The purpose of writing about an extract is to identify how Shakespeare creates dramatic effect. What techniques does he use?
- Try to imagine the action. Visualise the scene in your mind's eye. But remember there can be many valid ways of performing a scene. Offer alternatives. Justify your own preferences by reference to the language.
- What guides for actors' movement and expressions are given in the language? Comment on any stage directions.
- What is the importance of the extract in the play as a whole?
- How does the extract develop plot, reveal character, deepen themes?
- In what ways can the extract be spoken/staged to reflect a particular interpretation?
- How might an audience respond? In Elizabethan times? Today?

Writing an essay

As part of your study of *King Richard III* you will be asked to write essays, either under examination conditions or for coursework (term papers). Examinations mean that you are under pressure of time, usually having around one hour to prepare and write each essay. Coursework means that you have much longer to think about and produce your essay. But whatever the type of essay, each will require you to develop an argument about a particular aspect of *King Richard III*.

The essays you write on *King Richard III* require that you set out your thoughts on a particular aspect of the play, using evidence from the text. The people who read your essays (examiners, teachers, lecturers) will have certain expectations of your writing. In each essay they will expect you to discuss and analyse a particular topic, using evidence from the play to develop an argument in an organised, coherent and persuasive way. Examiners look for, and reward, what they call 'an informed personal response'. This simply means that you show you have good knowledge of the play ('informed') and use evidence from it to support and justify your own viewpoint ('personal').

You can write about *King Richard III* from different points of view. As pages 92–106 show, you can approach the play from a number of critical perspectives (feminist, political, psychoanalytic, etc.). You can also set the play in its social, literary, political and other contexts. You should write at different levels, moving beyond description to analysis and evaluation. Simply telling the story or describing characters is not as effective as analysing how events or characters embody wider concerns of the play – its preoccupations, or, more simply, what the play is about. In *King Richard III*, these wider concerns include power politics and the Tudor myth; nemesis and the cycle of revenge; the role of the individual conscience; Church versus state; appearance and reality.

How should you answer an examination question or write a coursework essay? The following threefold structure can help you organise your response:

opening paragraph
developing paragraphs
concluding paragraph.

Opening paragraph. Begin with a paragraph identifying just what topic or issue you will focus on. Show that you have understood what the question is about. You will have prepared for particular topics. But look closely at the question and identify key words to see what particular aspect it asks you to write about. Adapt your material to answer that question. Examiners do not reward an essay, however well written, if it is not on the question set.

Developing paragraphs. This is the main body of your essay. In it, you develop your argument, point by point, paragraph by paragraph. Use evidence from the play that illuminates the topic or issue, and answers the question set. Each paragraph makes a point of dramatic or thematic significance. Some paragraphs could make points concerned with context or particular critical approaches. The effect of your argument builds up as each paragraph adds to the persuasive quality of your essay. Use brief quotations that support your argument, and show clearly just why they are relevant. Ensure that your essay demonstrates that you are aware that *King Richard III* is a play; a drama intended for performance and, therefore, open to a wide variety of interpretations and audience responses.

Concluding paragraph. Your final paragraph pulls together your main conclusions. It does not simply repeat what you have written earlier, but summarises concisely how your essay has successfully answered the question.

Example

The following notes show the 'ingredients' of an answer. In an examination it is usually helpful to prepare similar notes from which you write your essay, paragraph by paragraph. To help you understand how contextual matters or points from different critical approaches might be included, the words 'Context' or 'Criticism' appear before some items (but would not appear in your essay). Remember that examiners are not impressed by 'name-dropping': use of critics' names. They want you to show your own knowledge and judgement of the play and its contexts, and your understanding of how it has been interpreted from different critical perspectives.

> Question: 'The women's roles in *King Richard III* are sometimes cut or reduced in performance. What does the play lose by such cuts or reductions?'

Opening paragraph

Show that you are aware that the question asks you to demonstrate your understanding of what is lost if the women's roles are cut or reduced in Shakespeare's text and then to give reasons for how important you feel the women are in the play. So you could include the following points and aim to write a sentence or more on each:

- *King Richard III* is described as a tragedy in the First Folio, so Richard's rise and fall is the central interest.
- Cibber's version established the tradition of cutting or greatly reducing the roles of Queen Elizabeth, the Duchess of York and Queen Margaret to create a star part for the actor playing Richard.
- But the women in the play are essential to the shape and balance of Shakespeare's argument and are crucial to the structure of the play.
- Criticism The feminine viewpoint provides a vital contrast to masculine power politics.

Developing paragraphs

Now write a paragraph on each of a number of different ways in which the play would lose its balance, structure and alternative viewpoints if women's roles were cut or lost. In each paragraph, identify the importance (dramatic, thematic, etc.) of the example you discuss. Some of the points you might include are given briefly below. One aspect of the importance of some of these is given in brackets, but there are of course others.

- Context Women are powerless in a hierarchical male world through a loss of status (death of husbands/sons) but find their voice to oppose Richard when he is king.
- Criticism: feminist The women oppose and expose Richard: the Duchess (Richard's birth); Margaret (curse); Elizabeth (her daughter marries Richmond, not Richard).
- Criticism: traditional Queen Margaret is an essential counter-

balance to Richard. Her role as nemesis links past and present and reminds audiences of former bloody deeds.

- Criticism: feminist Margaret teaches the Duchess of York and Queen Elizabeth to curse. They voice crucial opposition to Richard before Richmond's appearance, and are essential to Shakespeare's argument.

- Criticism: language The women use formal, ritualistic language and emphasise the classical origins of the drama that underpin the working out of the Tudor myth.

- Context The three scenes in which women appear reverse the Three Mary scenes of medieval morality plays (rejoicing becomes lamentation) and reinforce Richard's brutality.

- Criticism: psychoanalytic Women reveal Richard's inner life: Anne (Richard has 'timorous dreams'); Duchess (Richard's birth and maturity); Margaret (Richard's hellish origins).

- Criticism: psychoanalytic Richard's misogyny originates from maternal rejection. The double renunciation by women (Act 4 Scene 4) anticipates his physical defeat by Richmond.

- The women provide balance to the play's structure through parallel scenes: two wooing scenes; two cursing scenes; two scenes of lamentation.

- The women bring vital contrast in a play without a subplot through domestic scenes with children, providing pathos to expose Richard's brutal *realpolitik*.

Concluding paragraph
Write several sentences pulling together your conclusions. You might include the following points:

- Context Since Cibber's version, the importance of women's roles has become fully recognised. Women are essential to the balance, structure and argument of the play.

- Richard admits Queen Elizabeth and Jane Shore's influence over King Edward and Hastings and sneeringly observes that 'men are ruled by women'.

- Criticism: performance Queen Margaret is regarded by many actresses as one of Shakespeare's most versatile roles. She appears in all four plays (*Henry VI Parts 1, 2, 3* and *King Richard III*), ages thirty-five years and changes from beautiful young queen to vengeful old woman. Jane Shore, who does not appear in the play, often appears in film and stage productions which stress her power and influence.

- Criticism: traditional/feminist Elizabeth's political astuteness and opposition to Richard enables Richmond to marry Princess Elizabeth. This unites Lancastrians and Yorkists. The princess never appears on stage but lends legitimacy to Richmond.

Writing about character

Much critical writing about *King Richard III* traditionally focused on characters as if they were living human beings. Today it is not sufficient just to describe their personalities. When you write about characters you will also be expected to show that they are dramatic constructs, part of Shakespeare's stagecraft. They embody the wider concerns of the play, have certain dramatic functions, and are set in a social and political world with particular values and beliefs. They reflect and express issues of significance to Shakespeare's society – and today's.

All that may seem difficult and abstract. But don't feel overwhelmed. Everything you read in this book is written with those principles in mind, and can be a model for your own writing. Of course, you should say what a character seems like to you, but you should also write about how Shakespeare makes her or him part of his overall dramatic design.

A different way of thinking about character is that in Shakespeare's time, playwrights and audiences were less concerned with psychological realism than with character types and their functions. That is, they expected and recognised such stock figures of traditional drama as the foolish courtier; innocent children; duped lover; vengeful mother. Today, film and television have accustomed audiences to expect the inner life of characters to be revealed. Although Shakespeare's characters do reveal their inmost thoughts and feelings, especially in soliloquy, his audiences tended to regard them as characters in a developing story, to be understood by how they formed part of that story, and by how far they conformed to certain well-known types and fulfilled certain traditional roles.

In *King Richard III*, the chief protagonist dominates the play, and his character is the only one that is developed in detail. This is because the play chronicles his rise and fall. His character type is that of a bad and evil king who is conquered by a good and saintly opponent. Of the 25 scenes in the play, Richard appears in 15 and his unseen presence dominates the remaining ten. All the other characters in the play exist to dramatise his rise and fall or comment upon it.

But there is also a danger in writing about the functions of characters or the character types they represent. To reduce a character to a mere plot device is just as inappropriate as treating him or her as a real person. When you write about characters in *King Richard III* you should try to achieve a balance between analysing their personality, identifying the dilemmas they face, and placing them in their social, critical and dramatic contexts. That style of writing is found all through this Guide, and it can, together with the following brief discussions, help your own written responses to character.

Three men in the play are crucial in illustrating Richard's brutal rise to power. Clarence, Hastings and Buckingham in turn become victims of Richard's merciless plotting. Shakespeare exposes the ironies implicit in appearance and reality, as each is fooled and blinded by Richard's false friendship. Finally, just before execution, each man is forced by his conscience to examine his own moral nature.

Clarence

Clarence's first appearance emphasises his trusting faith in a scheming brother who is about to have him executed. Clarence's gullibility generates situations where irony is at once funny, and macabre. Richard's opening line to Clarence ('Brother, good day') creates a mocking, yet ominous tone that is sustained throughout Clarence's two appearances on stage. Moments before his death, Clarence tells the two murderers whom Richard has sent to kill him that Richard is loving and kindly and 'would labour my delivery', not realising that Richard is planning to deliver him from life rather than prison. Shakespeare underplays Clarence's involvement in past events (perjury and murder in *Henry VI Part 3*), focusing instead on his dream, where, in an episode rich in imagery, Clarence finds belief in Christianity and understands the power of conscience, repenting his past crimes.

As Clarence is the first of Richard's victims to die, his acceptance of the Christian principles of sin and salvation resonate throughout the play. Each of Richard's victims, like Clarence, faces the consequences of his past deeds. Richard's rejection before Bosworth of the Christian principles that Clarence has embraced stresses his isolation from man and God. Clarence's murder on stage is a rare example of explicit violence in the play, and underlines the brutal world of Richard's *realpolitik*.

Hastings

Imprisoned through the intrigues of the Woodvilles, Hastings is a faithful supporter of the house of York. But his loyalty is ineffective, for he possesses neither the political skill nor the insight into character so essential for survival in Richard's new, brutal world. His over-confidence and blindness to the real motives of others, allied to his bitter opposition to the Woodvilles, makes him an easy victim for Richard's plans. He rejoices at the executions of Rivers, Grey and Vaughan and is convinced of his own invincibility. But Hastings' misinterpretations of every warning sustain the grim irony that characterises the play. He fails to take the advice of Stanley to flee north, and he refuses Catesby's appeal to support Richard's bid for the crown. That Catesby's appeal is phrased in the most unambiguous terms (the opposite of Buckingham's instructions to find out 'as it were afar off') makes his blindness to his own perilous situation all the more astonishing. In a deeply ironic episode at the council, he believes that Richard is incapable of hiding his true feelings, and intends harm to no one present. Realising his fatal mistake too late, he recalls Margaret's curse as he prophesies 'the fearful'st time' for England under Richard. Like Clarence, he realises too late that he has relied on earthly success rather than God's grace.

Buckingham

Buckingham possesses those qualities that Hastings lacks, and his ability to dissemble almost rivals Richard's own. He possesses great political awareness and diplomatic skill and appears first as peacemaker, bringing messages from Edward IV to appease the various rivalries. Standing aloof from the bitter family arguments, Buckingham is the only important person not cursed by Margaret, but his neutrality evaporates when he seizes the opportunity to join with Richard in isolating Edward, Prince of Wales, from his family. He becomes Richard's right-hand man, and much of the humour and irony of Acts 2 and 3 derives from the energy and verve Buckingham and Richard generate as they embark on a spree of outrageous play-acting and stage-management which has such lethal outcomes. They order the imprisonment and execution of Rivers, Grey and Vaughan; send the princes to the Tower and contrive Hastings' execution; persuade the citizens of London there is a plot against them and fool the Mayor and aldermen into making Richard king. But Buckingham cannot bring himself to commit the final deed that Richard wants – the murder of the princes. His hesitation brings an abrupt end to their partnership. When Richard refuses to grant him the promised earldom of Hereford, Buckingham's reaction is unlike Hastings', for he does not hesitate. He raises an army against Richard, but a storm disperses his troops. Before his execution, he recognises the justice of his punishment and reflects that 'Margaret's curse falls heavy on my neck'.

Margaret's curse is an insistent reminder throughout the play of the power of nemesis and fate as characters face the inevitable consequences of their actions. Buckingham's fall within this pattern marks the beginning of Richard's own decline in fortune. The 'deep-revolving witty Buckingham' is replaced by the sinister figure of Ratcliffe. Richard will rely increasingly on several unprincipled men to carry out his brutal plans.

Stanley

Lord Stanley is the husband of Margaret Beaufort and stepfather to Richmond. Queen Elizabeth, who knows Stanley's wife hates all the Woodvilles, first challenges Stanley's loyalty. His reply is both tactful and politic, an approach he uses successfully throughout the play to avoid suspicion. His successful plea to Edward IV to save the life of his servant establishes Stanley as a caring master who is respected by the king. Stanley shows some of his true feelings when he warns Hastings to be suspicious of Richard, and later he encourages Dorset to join Richmond. Powerless to stop Richard becoming king, Stanley waits for an opportune moment. When Richard holds his son hostage and threatens him with execution, Stanley promises the tyrant military support. But he secretly intends to support Richmond. Using Richard's own weapons of double-dealing and hypocrisy, Stanley joins Richmond to defeat Richard and his son's life is spared.

Stanley gradually emerges as an important focus for opposition to Richard, aware almost from the beginning of Richard's true nature. He shows he is a true friend to the victims of Richard's regime, aiding

Dorset's escape and secretly assisting in Richmond's invasion. In the final act, Shakespeare uses Stanley to contrast brutal Richard, who tries to force Stanley to obedience, with honourable Richmond, whom Stanley addresses with genuine affection. Stanley plays Richard at his own game, his words hiding his true intentions, and it is his covert support of Richmond that is crucial to Richard's defeat.

Richmond

Richmond seems to be the all-conquering hero who ends Richard's evil reign. He appears to have all the right credentials: he is high-principled, honourable, moral, righteous, a fighter who wants only his country's good. Believing God will support his just cause, he puts his fate in God's hands. As he is not part of the bloody legacy of the Wars of the Roses, the ghosts acknowledge his innocence. An astute tactician who realises the importance of Stanley's forces, he shows genuine affection for his stepfather and is magnanimous in victory.

Resistance gathers against Richard in the second part of the play. It begins covertly with Stanley and later finds its voice through old Queen Margaret, the Duchess and Queen Elizabeth. Richmond's late appearance as a *deus ex machina* (a god who intervenes to resolve difficulties at the last moment) marks the culmination of that resistance, while the alternating scenes between Richard and Richmond's rival camps in Act 5 Scene 3 prepare the audience for Richard's inevitable downfall. Some commentators argue that Richmond is the hero saving England from Richard's oppression, but others disagree. They claim that the play has been starved of moral language for so long, while Richard has delighted audiences with his Machiavellian cunning, that the contest is not a fair one. Such transparent moral righteousness as Richmond possesses seems naive and dramatically less convincing against the much more interesting character of Richard.

Anne

Anne Neville was betrothed to Prince Edward, the son of King Henry VI, and she first appears mourning over Henry's corpse. Richard, who has killed both Edward and Henry, engages her in a war of words, resolved only when she agrees to become his queen. Later in the play, Anne shows courage and determination when she visits the princes in the Tower, challenging Brakenbury to allow her to enter. About to be crowned queen, she reveals that the curse she placed on Richard's future wife has ironically fallen upon her. Having been seduced by his 'honey words' at the start of the play, in almost her last utterance, she reveals her fear that he will 'shortly be rid of me'. She is right. He arranges her death so that he can marry the young Elizabeth.

The wooing scene portrays Richard at the height of his powers. He revels in his role of lover as he seeks to persuade the woman whose future father-in-law and husband he has murdered to become his wife. Shakespeare uses Anne as a dramatic device to reveal Richard's wit, deviousness and audacity at an early stage. The scene with Anne also establishes the contemptuous view of women that is an important feature of Richard's personality. Shakespeare typically juxtaposes one scene against another to bring out contrast. In the second wooing scene, Richard fails to convince Queen Elizabeth that he should marry her daughter. Critics point out that this demonstrates Richard's persuasive powers weakening and heralds his downfall. Anne also serves as a potent reminder of the power of cursing, as her curse on Richard is ironically visited on herself. While stressing Richard's brutal nature (she is right to fear for her life) she anticipates Richard's night of personal horror in facing the ghosts of all his victims by referring to his 'timorous dreams'.

A note on examiners

Examiners do not try to trap you or trick you. They set questions and select passages for comment intended to help you to write your own informed personal response to the play. They expect your answer to display a sound knowledge and understanding of the play, and to be well structured. They want you to develop an argument, using evidence from the text to support your interpretations and judgements. Examiners know there is never one 'right answer' to a question, but always opportunities to explore different approaches and interpretations. As such, they welcome answers that directly address the question set, and that demonstrate originality, insight and awareness of complexity. Above all, they reward responses that show your perception that *King Richard III* is a play for performance, and that you can identify how Shakespeare achieves his dramatic effects.

Resources

Books

Stephen M Buhler, 'Camp Richard III and the Burdens of (Stage/Film) History' in Mark Thornton Burnett and Ramona Wray (ed.), *Shakespeare, Film, Fin de Siècle*, Macmillan, 2000
An essay on the McKellen–Loncraine film.

Mark Thornton Burnett and Ramona Wray (ed.), *Shakespeare, Film, Fin de Siècle*, Macmillan, 2000
This collection of essays claims to identify how certain Shakespeare films engage with, and are relevant to, modern society (contains the essays by Buhler and Sinyard noted in this book list).

Irene G Dash, 'The Paradox of Power in *Richard III*' in Neil Taylor and Brian Loughrey (ed.), *Shakespeare's Early Tragedies: Richard III, Titus Andronicus, Romeo and Juliet*, Macmillan, 1990
A feminist interpretation of the role of the women in the play.

Jonathan Dollimore, *Radical Tragedy: Religion, Ideology and Power in the Drama of Shakespeare* (2nd edition), Harvester Wheatsheaf, 1989
Reinterprets Renaissance drama in the light of cultural materialism.

Juliet Dusinberre, *Shakespeare and the Nature of Women* (2nd edition), Macmillan, 1996
A key text in feminist approaches to Shakespeare. Dusinberre argues Shakespeare viewed men and women as equal.

Shirley Nelson Garner and Madelon Sprengnether (ed.), *Shakespearean Tragedy and Gender*, Indiana University Press, 1996
A collection of feminist criticism (contains the essay by Rackin mentioned below).

Graham Holderness, *Shakespeare: The Histories*, Macmillan, 2000
A challenging book that exemplifies the new historicism approach to Shakespeare.

Russell Jackson and Robert Smallwood (ed.), *Players of Shakespeare 3*, Cambridge University Press, 1993
Contains an account of Anton Lesser's views on playing Richard and those of Penelope Downie on the role of Margaret.

Frank Kermode, *Shakespeare's Language*, Allen Lane, Penguin, 2000
Contains only a brief section on *King Richard III*, but the discussion of the other tragedies can also help with an understanding of Shakespeare's use of language in this play.

L C Knights, 'Shakespeare: The Histories, Writers and Their Work', Longman, 1962
Contains a short essay about the politics of *King Richard III* and its structure.

Jan Kott, *Shakespeare Our Contemporary* (2nd edition), Methuen, 1967
Kott's working out of the 'Grand Mechanism' of history and accounts of performances of the play have had a major impact on many productions.

Ian McKellen, *William Shakespeare's Richard III: A Screenplay*, Doubleday, 1996

John Julius Norwich, *Shakespeare's Kings*, Viking, 1999
Helpful reading for an understanding of the interplay between history and the history plays.

Keith Parsons and Pamela Mason (ed.), *Shakespeare in Performance*, Salamander, 1995
Contains a summary of some of the most dramatic moments in performances of the play in the late twentieth century.

Phyllis Rackin, 'History into Tragedy: The Case of *Richard III*' in Shirley Nelson Garner and Madelon Sprengnether (ed.), *Shakespearean Tragedy and Gender*, Indiana University Press, 1996
A strongly argued feminist view about the marginalising of the women in *King Richard III*.

Peter Reynolds, 'Acting *Richard III*' in Neil Taylor and Brian Loughrey (ed.), *Shakespeare's Early Tragedies: Richard III, Titus Andronicus, Romeo and Juliet*, Macmillan, 1990
Performance criticism about the wooing of Anne scene.

A P Rossiter, *Angel with Horns, and Other Shakespearean Lectures*, Longman Group Ltd, 1961
Contains a very influential essay that challenges the idea of the Tudor myth and emphasises the humour in the play.

Peter Saccio, *Shakespeare's English Kings: History, Chronicle and Drama*, Oxford University Press, 1977
An explanation of how history was used by Shakespeare in the history plays.

Antony Sher, *Year of the King*, Methuen Drama, 1985
A fascinating account of Sher's preparations for his acclaimed performance of Richard with the Royal Shakespeare Company.

Neil Sinyard, 'Shakespeare meets the Godfather: The Postmodern Populism of Al Pacino's *Looking for Richard*' in Mark Thornton Burnett and Ramona Wray (ed.), *Shakespeare, Film, Fin de Siècle*, Macmillan, 2000
Argues that Pacino's film demystifies and deconstructs Shakespeare.

Caroline Spurgeon, *Shakespeare's Imagery and What it Tells Us*, Cambridge University Press, 1935
The first major study of imagery in the plays. Spurgeon's identification of image-clusters as a dominant feature of the plays has influenced all later studies.

Neil Taylor and Brian Loughrey (ed.), *Shakespeare's Early Tragedies: Richard III, Titus Andronicus, Romeo and Juliet*, Macmillan, 1990
Contains the essays by Dash and Reynolds noted in this book list, as well as passages from the books by Rossiter and Tillyard and other valuable extracts about the play from pre-twentieth-century critics.

E M W Tillyard, *Shakespeare's History Plays*, Chatto and Windus, 1944
Very thorough on the sources of Shakespeare's history plays; clearly explains the Tudor myth.

Derek Traversi, *An Approach to Shakespeare*, Hollis and Carter, 1968
Contains thought-provoking insights into the character of Richard and the structure of the play.

Films

The three films listed below are usually obtainable on video or DVD.

Richard III (UK, 1955) Director: Laurence Olivier. Laurence Olivier (Richard III).

Richard III (UK, 1995) Director: Richard Loncraine. Ian McKellen (Richard III).

Looking for Richard (USA, 1997) Director: Al Pacino. Al Pacino (Richard III).

Other videos of the play:

- *Richard III* (BBC, UK, 1982) Director: Jane Howell. Ron Cook (Richard III).
  Made as part of the BBC television Shakespeare series.

- *Richard III* (Portman Productions (The English Shakespeare Company), UK, 1990) Director: Michael Bogdanov. Andrew Jarvis (Richard III).
  A video of a long-running stage version.

- *Richard III* (USA, 1912). Frederick Ward (Richard III).
  Unlikely to be readily available today!

Audio books

HarperCollins (King Richard III: Robert Stephens)

Naxos (King Richard III: Kenneth Branagh)

Penguin (King Richard III: David Troughton)